Writing 150 Course Book

2018–2019

THE WRITING PROGRAM

UNIVERSITY OF SOUTHERN CALIFORNIA

macmillan learning
curriculum solutions

Printed in the United States of America

10 9 8 7 6 5 4 3 2 1

ISBN 978-1-5339-0703-5

Macmillan Learning Curriculum Solutions
14903 Pilot Drive
Plymouth, MI 48170
www.macmillanlearning.com

Rivera 0703-5 F18

Sustainability
Hayden-McNeil's standard paper stock uses a minimum of 30% post-consumer waste. We offer higher % options by request, including a 100% recycled stock. Additionally, Hayden-McNeil Custom Digital provides authors with the opportunity to convert print products to a digital format. Hayden-McNeil is part of a larger sustainability initiative through Macmillan Learning. Visit http://sustainability.macmillan.com to learn more.

bedford/st. martin's • hayden-mcneil
w.h. freeman • worth publishers

USC Dana and David Dornsife College of Letters, Arts and Sciences
Writing Program Faculty and Staff

Writing Program Directors

Norah Ashe-McNalley
Director

Mariko Dawson Zare
Associate Director

Jeffrey Chisum
Associate Director

Cory Elizabeth Nelson
Writing Center Director

Administrative Staff

Jasmine Robledo, Project Specialist—Administrative
Lilyan Lam, Administrative Assistant
Lettie Littlejohn, Administrative Assistant
Roger Anderson, Assistant Director of the Writing Center

Writing Program Faculty

Pamela Albanese
Emily Artiano
Jennifer Bankard
Christina Belcher
Justin Bibler
Tamara Black
Amanda Bloom
Diana Blaine
Stephanie Bower
Ryan Boyd
Mike Bunn
Jessica Cantiello
LauraAnne Carroll-Adler
Brent Chappelow
Jeff Chisum
James Clements
James Condon
April Davidauskis
Andrew De Silva
Carlos Delgado
Daniel Dissinger
Elizabeth Durst
Antonio Elefano
William Feuer
Jay Fisher

Laurie Fisher
Amber Foster
Mary Glavan
Rochelle Gold
Brett Gordon
William Gorski
Farida Habeeb
Devon Harlow
Amanda Hobmeier
Taiyaba Husain
Jessi Johnson
Nathalie Joseph
Ashley Karlin
Shana Kraynak
Meridith Kruse
Alexis Landau
Kate Levin
Rory Lukins
Stephen Mack
Matthew Manson
Mark Marino
P.T. McNiff
Sarah Mesle
Amy Meyerson
Dana Milstein

Indra Mukhopadhyay
John Murray
Erika Nanes
Cory Elizabeth Nelson
Vanessa Osborne
Benjamin Pack
Leah Pate
Stephanie Payne
Daniel Pecchenino
Jessica Piazza
Steve Posner
Shefali Rajamannar
Eric Rawson
DeAnna Rivera
Sandra Ross
Alisa Sanchez
Atia Sattar
Anne Schindel
Deborah Sims
Scott Smith
David Tomkins
Mary Traester
Robert Waller, Jr.
Ellen Wayland-Smith
Yance Wyatt

Assistant Lecturers

Samantha Cohen	Emily Geminder	Teddy Lance
Petrina Crockford	Muriel Leung	Zachary Torp
Sara Fetherolf	Vanessa Villarreal	

CONTRIBUTORS

John Holland

The wisdom of John Holland, who gracefully steered the Writing Program for so many years, lies at the heart of the *Writing 150 Course Book*. John empowered writing instructors by giving us the space to develop and refine our own teaching styles while guiding us toward the best Rhetoric and Composition practices. At the same time, he was cannily modeling the ethical treatment of our students, whom, in a similar way, we encourage to discover their own voices, their own arguments, while challenging them to think critically and navigate the academic scene. John's vision of a simultaneously humane and rigorous writing pedagogy informs this course book as it does the program as a whole now and for years to come.

Jack Blum

Jack Blum's passion for all things Rhetoric and Composition fueled the genesis and continued growth of this course book. His fiery willingness to argue, learn, argue again, and learn more served as the founding example for the rest of the contributors listed below to do the same. His inspiring contributions will reverberate always.

Materials, concepts, and suggestions for the *Writing 150 Course Book* were contributed by the following members, past and present, of the Writing Program's instructional staff.

Elizabeth Bleicher	Des Harding	Mark Richardson
Jason Bostick	Peter Huk	DeAnna Rivera
Amy Braden	Joan Jastrebski	Ned Schantz
Peter Brau	Sheilah Jones	Nikki Senecal
Elizabeth Brown	Valerie Karno	Eric Rawson
John Bruns	Kimberlee Keeline	Ishita Sinha Roy
LauraAnne Carroll-Adler	Kristiane Keller	R. Scott Smith
Kris Deffenbacher	Kevin Laam	Rob Sturr
Andrew De Silva	Glenn Libby	Romy Taylor
Francene Engel	Kim Manner	Mary Beth Tegan
Molly Engelhardt	Mark Masterson	Anne Thorpe
Kenneth Evans	Marya McFadden	Mary Traester
William Feuer	Indra Mukhopadhyay	Trisha Tucker
Dean Franco	John Murray	Robert Waller, Jr.
Michael Frisoli	Cory Elizabeth Nelson	Rosemary Weatherston
Shadi Ganjavi	Amy Obrist	Jen Welsh
Royce Grubic	Michael O'Malley	Holly Van Houten
Roger Gustafson	Alina Orlov	Laura Scavuzzo Wheeler
Elizabeth Guzik	Vanessa Osborne	L. Bryan Williams
Rebecca Hanft	Athena Perrakis	Yance Wyatt
Farida Habeeb	Jennifer Raphael	Sean Zwagerman
	Mike Reynolds	

Table of Contents

PART III. STUDENT GUIDE TO WRITING 150

General Introduction: Writing 150

Welcome to Writing 150, the initial course in the composition sequence at the University of Southern California. Writing 150 provides a foundation of general writing competence in support of your undergraduate studies. In your junior year, you will complete the composition sequence by taking Writing 340, an upper-division course that focuses more specifically upon the writing practices of your own disciplinary or professional area.

Writing 150 will help you develop the thinking and writing skills necessary for success in General Education and major courses while inviting you to join a broader, on-going academic and cultural conversation. You will be encouraged to acquire information and ideas not simply as material for examinations, but as "equipment for living" in both the academic context and beyond, thereby, becoming an active, self-directed, lifelong learner. Although different versions of Writing 150 will address different themes, each thematic group will provide a context in which you can apply academic concepts in the exploration of issues relevant to you and your generation.

Writing 150 is offered in various **thematic groups** intended to appeal to a range of student interests and to allow students access to a wide range of genuine and compelling issues: e.g., "Issues in Sustainability," "Globalization: Current Issues and Cross-Cultural Perspectives," "Health and Healing," "Technology and Social Change," "Education and Intellectual Development," etc. The various themes are not intended to correspond to any one General Education category; rather, the themes resonate across multiple categories and are thus relevant to students from diverse Dornsife and professional majors. For example, a "Technology and Social Change" group delves into concepts that are consistent with perspectives presented in General Education courses from the sciences, social sciences, quantitative reasoning, and the arts and humanities.

Course Purpose and Personal Motivation

Many college classes are "content" courses designed to present a particular body of knowledge and to foster opportunities for students to gain familiarity with key concepts and theories from that content area. By contrast, writing classes concentrate on praxis: their purpose is to help students develop and improve certain skills and practices. In a writing course, what counts is not so much what you know about writing, but what you can do as a writer.

Because your success in Writing 150 will depend largely upon effort and practice, motivation becomes an important issue. While grades may provide some impetus in this regard, they are ultimately an indirect form of motivation. There are more significant reasons for improving your writing skills.

For one thing, effective writing will be an asset to you in the majority of courses you take at the university; writing can significantly enhance your overall performance as a student. No matter how well you have mastered the content of a course, your understanding and insights will count for little unless you are able to articulate them effectively. The communicative importance of writing is likely to become even more crucial once you graduate, for writing ability is a key factor of success in most fields or professions. To move beyond entry-level positions, you will need to use writing to convince others of the merits of your proposals and to coordinate the activities of those you supervise. Even in technical fields such as engineering, the further you advance in your career, the more time you are likely to spend in formal written communication.

In addition to these instrumental considerations, however, writing has a significance that is often overlooked and that is perhaps even more vital. Beyond its importance as a means of communication, writing has an **epistemological** function: it is in itself a powerful means of knowing and learning.

When you write about a topic, you make discoveries and connections that were not initially apparent to you, that take you beyond the passive reception of ideas that you gain through lectures or readings. Writing allows you to integrate and critique the knowledge you have acquired, and thus to grasp it more firmly. In ten years' time, you may recall few of the questions you faced on multiple-choice tests in college, but you are much more likely to remember concepts and arguments that you proposed in your own papers.

Pedagogical Themes of Writing 150: Critical Reasoning, Invention, Arrangement, Style, and Revision

Writing is an exceptionally complex activity. Within the university, writing projects are likely to involve not only linguistic competence (grammar, syntax, diction, etc.) but topical knowledge, organizational ability, research skills, social and cultural understanding, rhetorical judgment, and—most important of all—insight, thought, and creativity.

The complexity of college writing is reflected in the course objectives for Writing 150 listed in Part III of the *Course Book*. While you will want to review these goals and become familiar with them, the course can probably be more easily understood in terms of five principal pedagogical themes—critical reasoning, invention, arrangement, style, revision—that together cover almost everything you will be asked to do in Writing 150.

The first theme, **critical reasoning**, addresses the development of skills having to do with critical thinking, analysis, and argumentation, as these abilities will be most important to the sorts of writing that is required in university courses and later as part of your professional and civic responsibilities.

Critical reasoning includes:

> the ability to move beyond the limits of one's initial ideas and presuppositions about a topic;

> the techniques used both to support and to question argumentative claims;

> the development of intellectual skepticism and honesty, and tolerance for opposing viewpoints.

The next three themes—**invention, arrangement**, and **style**—are closely related and represent three of the five principal arts of classical rhetoric. Memory and delivery, the other two elements of classical rhetoric, have to do with oral discourse—speeches—and so have less relevance to a course in written composition, but invention, arrangement, and style remain fundamental to any writing project.

Invention includes:

> the generation of new ideas and perspectives on an issue;

> the use of inscriptive methods—freewriting, listing, clustering, etc.—to track ideas more effectively;

> the application of heuristics, techniques that may be applied to a topic to elicit insights and concepts.

Arrangement includes:

> the review of prewriting materials and the selection of potentially useful ideas and arguments;

> the creation of a plan or structure around which to base a provisional argument;

> the determination of an effective sequence for the main points of an argument or analysis.

Style includes:

> all matters of word choice and sentence formation;

> the ability to use the surface features of a text—diction and syntax—to reinforce the text's purpose.

Invention, arrangement, and style are crucial to the process of writing. The same may be said of **revision**, the fifth pedagogical theme of Writing 150. Revision encompasses all of the conceptual and formal adjustments and modifications that must be accomplished in order to produce a sound final draft.

Revision includes:

> reconsidering the purpose of the text, as well as the concepts and arguments so as to reflect this purpose more effectively;

> reexamining and modifying the large-scale structure of a draft;

> closely reviewing and adjusting the grammatical and stylistic elements of each sentence of the text.

To help you practice and improve upon these pedagogical themes, you will have many opportunities to undertake informal **ancillary writing** activities while working on a given assignment. The majority of ancillary writing will be directly related to the assignment and thus will provide a means to keep you on pace and to prepare you for class discussions and activities.

Ancillary writing might include journal entries or short editorials meant to establish your initial impressions on an issue, writing in creative genres that will enhance and inform your engagement in your academic work, peer reviews of other students' written work, and reflective writing following the submission of a formal essay. But, the ancillary writing will also serve other functions, encouraging you to engage with the academic life available at the university. You might, for example, be asked to attend one of the many lectures or workshops or cultural events offered each week and to think and write about how ideas encountered in that context may be related to an issue you are addressing in your writing class.

Regardless of the form it takes, the primary function of ancillary writing is to provide you with a venue in which to experience the epistemic power of writing—the way in which writing not only records ideas, but, in doing so, serves to generate new ones. In this light you will be encouraged to make note of information and ideas from a wide range of sources—newspapers, journals, books, substantive blog sites, etc.—and then connect observations to ideas and ideas to issues. Part III of the *Course Book* explains how these activities factor into your overall grade.

Instructional Approaches: Dialogue, Workshops, and Conferences

Along with knowing the principal themes of Writing 150, you will also find it useful to understand the instructional approaches that will be followed in your composition section. Unlike many content courses that must, because of their large enrollments, depend primarily upon lecture-based pedagogy, the Writing Program stresses **dialogue** as the basis for instruction. This emphasis means that students are expected to participate fully and responsibly in the discussions and activities of their writing class, not only in terms of interactions with their instructor but also with their classmates.

To encourage dialogue and interaction, the Writing Program uses writing **workshops** as the principal mode of instruction. Since writing is something you *do*, not just something you need to know about, writing workshops will allow you to practice the skills you will be expected to master. During workshop sessions, you will participate in a variety of reading and writing activities—discussing topics, generating ideas, drafting and revising essays, and analyzing your own writing and that of other students. Although occasional brief lectures may be used to present specific material, the majority of class time in Writing 150 will be spent in workshop sessions, so you should come to class each day prepared to participate, not just listen. To participate effectively, you should plan to keep up with the readings and other homework, have your drafts and other writing projects ready on time, and come to class prepared to raise questions and exchange ideas with your instructor and other students.

Along with your participation in writing workshops, you will also take part in four writing **conferences** of various kinds. Some of these will be one-to-one conferences with your instructor; others may be group conferences in which the instructor meets with several students together. In either case, the objective is to increase the feedback that students receive on their writing and to offer further opportunities for dialogue and interaction. An additional forum for instruction and interaction is provided by the Writing Center, where students can go to receive assistance on any aspect of the writing process. The last section in Part III of the *Course Book* explains how to make the best use of the Writing Center.

Rhetoric and Social Issues

Since composition classes are designed to promote the development of strong rhetorical skills, it is important to recall that the subject of rhetoric has a far longer and a much different history than many people realize. In common parlance, the term **rhetoric** is frequently employed in a derogatory manner, one that associates it with the *mis*use of language, with ways of speaking or writing that are deceptive or false. Politicians, for example, are often quick to dismiss their opponent's claims as "mere rhetoric" or to assert their own desire to "cut through the rhetoric" in order to address the "real issues" under consideration.

The irony to this, of course, is that rhetoric as a subject of study developed precisely *because* of the need to address "real" issues, those arising with the origin of democracy in Athens during the fifth century BC. The new Athenian government had two features that made it vital for citizens to be able to speak and argue effectively. For one thing, any citizen could participate in the assembly, debating public matters and perhaps even serving in public office. For another, within the newly instituted court system citizens had to argue legal cases for themselves, there being, for better or worse, no equivalent to our own system of legal counsel. The study of rhetoric began as a means by which Athenian citizens could prepare themselves to take on these civic duties.

Thus rhetoric has, from the start, been associated with the need to analyze and resolve social issues, and in this function it has always been closely linked to the fortunes of democracy. While it is certainly true that rhetorical ability, like any other skill, may be used in a dishonest or destructive manner, it would be naïve to condemn rhetoric on these grounds as a form of linguistic manipulation. There is a rhetorical dimension to any use of language, and the important question is whether the rhetorical context within a culture permits or precludes open and critical discourse.

It is therefore appropriate that Writing 150 is taught along thematic lines, for any thematic contains numerous debates and any debate numerous arguments. The skills of argument and analysis that you practice and develop in college will of course be important to both your academic and professional careers, but your understanding of rhetoric and your ability to distinguish legitimate and illegitimate rhetorical conduct may have larger implications as well. The quality of rhetorical practices within a culture has a great deal to do with the ethical and intellectual characteristics of that culture. Totalitarian societies are unlikely to arise in a rhetorical context that remains open, fair, and critical; free societies cannot be sustained in a rhetorical context that does not.

An Overview of the Writing Process

Writing 150 uses a **process approach** to foster the development of writing skills. While it certainly pays attention to the features of writing as a textual product, it is even more concerned with the activities writers undertake in the process of generating a text. Underlying this approach is the notion that in order to improve *what* you write you need to improve *how* you write.

As Diagram 1 indicates, however, the process of writing is always situated within a context that necessarily involves the expectations both of a **reader** and a larger **discourse community**. It is within a discourse community that we negotiate what counts or does not count as true or valid, and what is or is not accepted as appropriate discourse behavior. While it is obvious that discourse communities overlap, membership in any particular discourse community nevertheless depends upon sharing its epistemological assumptions and mastering its discourse conventions. All this bears directly on composition because the university itself constitutes an important discourse community, one which contains many sub-communities (these sub-communities may be suggested to some extent by the distinct thematic groups).

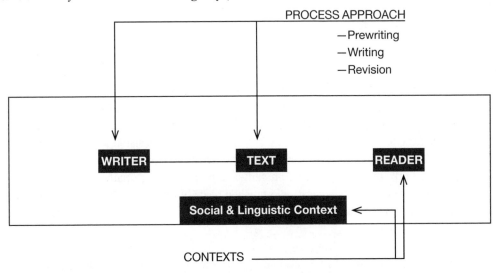

Diagram 1.

Improving writing skills and developing an effective writing process thus also means learning to be attuned to your reader's needs and expectations. On this view, a text is not so much a container of information that the reader simply and rather passively "un-packs" as it is a transaction between the writer's understanding and the reader's. From a transactional perspective, the reader has not only to unpack the information in a text, but also to reassemble it in such a way as to reach an understanding that is closely coherent to the writer's intention. In support of this transaction, the writer must therefore provide the reader with careful cues as to how the information in the text is to be interpreted and must also carefully identify and revise any sections of the text that may be obvious to the writer but unfamiliar or incomprehensible to the reader.

Your development as a writer will also entail becoming more familiar with the conventions and expectations—both formal and conceptual—of the academic discourse community which you now have joined. Although the individual disciplines within the university—the English department, the cinema school, the business school—have their own unique assumptions and conventions, there are also more general standards for writing that will be expected in any university course. Your texts, for example, will be expected to display, among other features, carefully reasoned arguments backed by plausible support, effective use of outside source material, and an academic style and tone.

The Process of Writing

Writing is a complex activity, one that is practiced in different contexts for different purposes by different writers, and so it follows that there can be no single or ideal model of "the" writing process. Diagram 2 (on the following page) is thus intended not to define some fool-proof system for generating effective writing but instead, and more modestly, only to illustrate many of the stages and activities that have proven characteristic of the writing processes of capable writers in many disciplines much (but not all) of the time.

To improve the effectiveness of your own writing, you might do well to consider how your own proclivities as a writer match up to the practices suggested in Diagram 2. Here two factors may be of particular importance.

One is balance of effort. Studies of the composing process have shown that effective writers tend to spend more time in the pre-writing stage, playing around with ideas and possible approaches to arrangement before getting down to an actual first draft. By contrast, weaker writers tend to spend less time on activities having to do with invention, selection, and planning, and instead show a preference for beginning a first draft after very little preparation. Proficient writers also tend to spend more time on revision than do weaker writers, and their revision focuses on large-scale changes as well as on surface-level editing. Less experienced writers spend less time on revision, and usually concentrate their attention on sentence-level editing. Finally, strong writers also spend more time overall when generating a finished piece of text, even though, once again, the perception among less proficient writers is that capable writers can "do it quicker," spending less time than they themselves do.

A second factor to keep in mind when evaluating your own writing process is **recursiveness**, the quality that is indicated in Diagram 2 by the arrows running both up and down between the major stages of prewriting, drafting, and revision. Proficient writers tend not to plow through the writing process in a simple linear sequence but instead are more likely to bounce back and forth between activities, revising a bit in the middle of their first draft, returning to invention activities when they get stuck in a draft or find a new idea during revision, and drafting new sections of text even after they have the rest of the piece proofread and polished. The messiness and unpredictability of such recursiveness account for the impossibility of constructing a single model of the writing process, but it is precisely these qualities that make writing a creative activity and that produce the most thoughtful and engaging texts.

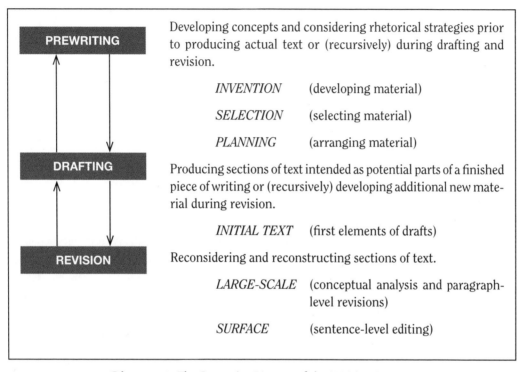

Diagram 2. The Recursive Nature of the Writing Process

Because the effectiveness of an entire paper depends upon the quality of its ideas, **prewriting** is a crucial part of a writing process. Prewriting is typically thought of as work writers do in developing ideas and plans for a paper *before* they begin to produce any text; however, the need for prewriting rarely disappears after this initial stage. Many writers find it necessary to come up with additional concepts and consider new strategies during drafting and revision. At any stage of the writing process, the goal of prewriting should be to move beyond initial or obvious responses to an issue and generate fresh, interesting material.

The heart of prewriting is invention—the discovery or creation of ideas and supporting materials to use in a paper. The invention process usually starts with the recollection of familiar information about a topic. To record and organize this information, you may use **inscriptive methods** (i.e., techniques for recording ideas) such as **listing**, **clustering**, or **freewriting**. The next step in invention is typically to generate a more extensive set of ideas and relationships while at the same time refining your thinking about the topic. One way to do this is with heuristics, methods of discovering new ideas. Several heuristics, including the **Fact/Idea List**, the **Pentad**, and the **Topics**, will be illustrated in *Section 2: Invention*.

These inventional and inscriptive techniques are essential components of any writing process. The more time you can spend creating, testing, and experimenting with ideas, the better your paper is likely to be. Keep in mind that experienced writers may spend as much as half their time on prewriting activities.

Along with inventing material, prewriting also involves selection and planning. Once you have developed a full and complex set of ideas, arguments, and information, it helps to spend time selecting the best of the material you have generated and coming up with an organizational strategy. While it's impossible to foresee every detail of a paper, having a well-thought-out plan will usually facilitate the next step: drafting.

Drafting starts when you begin to transform your notes and plans into paragraphs. During this stage, you should strive to balance the creation and the revision of text. If you have an idea, write it down, even if it's not polished. You don't want to become so focused on perfecting each idea and paragraph that completing a draft becomes a struggle. You'll want to give yourself time to do multiple drafts—while there's no right number, you'll probably find that you'll need more than one. You'll also benefit from time off between drafts, which allows you to review what you've written with a fresher perspective.

As you undertake **revision**, your knowledge of the writer–reader transaction becomes particularly important because you must shift from **writer-based language** (which reflects your private insight into a topic) to **reader-based language** (which provides sufficient cues to make your insights clear to readers). You must also be able to analyze your paper with both **surface-level** and **global** changes in mind. In addition to correcting grammatical and stylistic problems (surface-level concerns), you'll need to reflect upon the main concepts in your paper and determine whether there are more substantive matters to address (e.g., refining your thesis, re-cueing paragraphs, generating new material). Keep in mind, as you do, that professional writers always revise. Their seemingly effortless prose is the product of multiple drafts, which are scrutinized by the writers and their editors and friends.

How to Use This Book

The *Writing 150 Course Book* consists of three sections. Part I is divided into five subsections, each corresponding to an important instructional theme within the Writing 150 curriculum: **Critical Reasoning**, **Invention**, **Arrangement**, **Style**, and **Revision**. Insofar as writing is a recursive process, these sections may be used or assigned in almost any order, and your instructor will probably refer to and return to the resources contained in each section at various points throughout the semester.

Most of the writing you will do in the university is **intertextual**: the texts that you compose will necessarily draw from and comment upon other relevant texts. Part II of the *Course Book*, "Working with Outside Sources," explains the conventions and procedures requisite to effective intertextual writing at the university.

Part III of the *Course Book*, "The Student Guide to Writing 150," contains an overview of the Writing Program and information you will need throughout your enrollment in the course. This section describes important program and university policies and resources, explains grading procedures, and informs you of your rights and responsibilities regarding such matters as attendance and academic integrity.

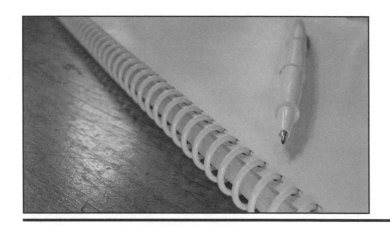

Part 1

RHETORICAL LESSONS AND ACTIVITIES

SECTION 1: Critical Reasoning, Analysis, and Argumentation

SECTION 2: Invention

SECTION 3: Arrangement

SECTION 4: Style

SECTION 5: Revision

Critical Reasoning, Analysis, and Argumentation

Critical Reasoning

Critique or critical reasoning is one of the principal themes of Writing 150 because the abilities to read, analyze, and think in a critical manner are crucial to successful college writing. It is therefore important to have an understanding of the critical attitude that underlies and defines much academic discourse.

In dealing with these sorts of complex issues, what counts is the ability to distinguish what is sound from what is false and to propose what can and should be done—the core objectives of critical reasoning. Such reasoning reflects two key values: intellectual skepticism and intellectual honesty. Intellectual skepticism is alert and charitable; it requires that good reasons and evidence be provided even for positions it favors, and it does not unfairly discount reasons and evidence provided in support of opposing positions. Intellectual honesty represents a willingness to admit errors and flaws in one's own position and to recognize the legitimate strengths of opposing arguments.

Nor should "critical thinking" be reduced to the ability to "solve" a problem that has only one correct answer. Critical thinking does involve problem solving, but it also requires the ability to apply reason to complex situations where conflicting concepts, values, and interests do not afford a clear, simple, and correct answer.

Analysis

Analysis has to do with close and careful inspection. The term analysis means to break something down into its constituent elements. A less-talked about component to analysis, however, is the notion that once something is broken down it must also be put back together. In writing which employs critical reasoning, writers break down an issue—a point about which reasonable minds would differ—and then put that idea together again for the reader using newly found perspectives gained through the writing and critical reasoning process. Most of the significant writing you will do in college or professional life will challenge you to move beyond the initial appearances of an issue and to investigate it in detail and from a critical perspective that will generate creative insights and understandings that were not at first apparent. The sections that follow discuss a number of topics—critical reading practices, the testing of validity claims and argumentative structures, and the identification of logical fallacies—that will assist in this regard.

Critical Reading Habits

Before addressing what it means to read critically, it may be useful first to consider on a more fundamental level what it means to read effectively in college. Texts must always be interpreted within a context, and being unfamiliar with the appropriate contextual or background information can lead to misinterpretation and misunderstanding.

It follows that you will need an approach to reading that will not only handle the increased reading load but also help you construct the conceptual frameworks necessary for successful understanding. This means that many students may find it necessary to modify their approach to reading. The standard model of reading, in which you begin with the first sentence of a text and read through to the last, is often not efficient enough to permit you to keep up with the reading load. More importantly, this approach to reading may make it more difficult to construct appropriate interpretive frameworks necessary to understand challenging and less familiar texts. If you still rely primarily upon the traditional first-sentence-to-last model of reading, you may be able to improve your reading efficiency by making use of one or more of the following techniques:

Pre-read the text. Before you begin closely reading a text, flip through it to get an initial sense of its topic, purpose, main ideas, and the attitude or position of its author. Read through the conclusion to see where the text is heading and try to identify sections you already understand or find interesting, as these may provide better "entry points" into the text than the introduction itself. Once you've pre-read the text in this manner, go back and give it a more thorough reading. Make sure you cover the entire text and understand it, but remember that you don't necessarily have to read it in any particular order.

Skip past sections you don't understand. You don't have to understand every single part of a text to understand the whole. If you encounter a sentence or two or even a paragraph that you don't understand, try "bouncing over" the problem and continuing your reading. You may find that a later part of the text clarifies the part you don't understand, or that you can grasp the gist of the argument without the aid of the incomprehensible material. Once you have a better overall understanding of the text, return to the puzzling section and see if you can figure it out.

Read economically. A text containing a relatively familiar argument, one for which you already have a strong contextual background, does not usually have to be read with the intensity or thoroughness of one presenting an unfamiliar argument. A text illustrating a theory may not require as close a reading as one presenting the theory itself. You have only a certain amount of study time and you need to manage it so that more difficult and/or central texts receive the time and care necessary to achieve close understanding.

Read purposefully and actively. Just as you are more likely to learn a game by playing it than by watching it, you are more likely to understand a text if you engage it actively rather than passively. Try to approach the text in terms of your own purposes as reader, searching for information that is most relevant to those specific purposes; this can help to provide a better context for your reading. Respond to the text by marking it up and writing comments in the margins.

Take concise notes of main points and key information. You won't be able to make a complete outline or record full notes for every book or article you are assigned to read. Instead, try to record at least brief notes on everything you do read, and collect these in a centralized form so that you may review them. Doing so will not only refresh your memory as to the important points of each text, but it will also help you develop the kind of conceptual background or context that will make you a better reader of other texts in that field.

Validity Claims

The suggestions offered on the previous page are directed toward making reading more effective in terms of identifying what a text is claiming, and as such, they may help to provide a basis for critical reading.

But critical reading itself goes beyond the recognition of what a text is "about" to test the validity of the information it provides and the arguments it proposes. In conducting a critical reading, it is therefore useful to have an analytical framework that can guide the examination of the text's validity. By distinguishing separate kinds of validity problems, this framework sharpens the analysis.

The framework is easy to use once you develop some familiarity with its four validity claims. As you re-read the text, look for parts of the text that are difficult for you to understand and/or agree with. Try to link each problem you identify with the validity claim that you believe it violates. When you finish your analysis, you will have a clear sense of *where* you agree or disagree with the text, a much better understanding of *why* you agree or disagree, and, perhaps most importantly, an appreciation for the kinds of questions or arguments you may wish to raise in response to areas of disagreement or uncertainty.

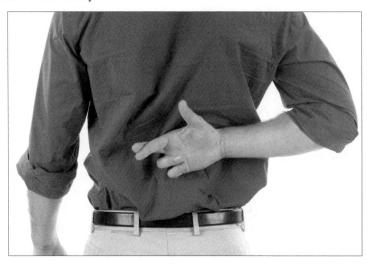

Validity Claim 1: Intelligibility/Comprehensibility

Is the text intelligible?

For example, if you do not speak Russian, then you are likely to find a text written in that language to be highly unintelligible. But even a text written in English—or in any other language you speak—may contain patches that are incomprehensible to you, with obscure terms, foreign phrases, and allusions to contextual knowledge with which you have no familiarity.

To resolve or critique: First determine whether the unintelligibility arises from your own side or the author's. If the text contains a word you don't know or a phrase from another language, this may be resolved simply by consulting a reference work. If, however, the text seems to you to be written in a manner that is deliberately incomprehensible or that uses an opaque style to cloak a threadbare argument, then you may have grounds for criticism.

Validity Claim 2: Truth

Are any facts, data, or evidence incorrect or false?

Even if a text is completely clear and intelligible, it may contain errors of fact. Make note of any factual information that you know or suspect to be incorrect. In addition to such false information, you should also look for evidence or data that appear implausible or highly unlikely.

To resolve or critique: Violations of the validity claim to factual truth are resolved or critiqued by identifying and explaining the factual error. In some cases this may be done with reference to general knowledge—you don't need to cite the *Encyclopedia Britannica* to convince most people that Canada is not part of Europe. Where the violation involves information that is not in the domain of common knowledge, counter-information from appropriate authorities should be consulted.

In cases where the violation seems to involve implausibility, the most effective critique is still to demonstrate factual error. If you are not able to locate the counter-information that would permit such refutation, you may still make a strong critique by carefully explaining why the data or evidence is highly unlikely to be true.

Validity Claim 3: Truthfulness or Sincerity

Does the text offer claims or arguments that are untruthful or unsound?

Even if a text is intelligible and has its facts in order, it may still make claims that are untruthful or unsound. Here it is useful to distinguish between claims that are clearly false from those that are unsound or invalid because of an unintentional flaw in reasoning.

In looking for deliberately false arguments, be particularly alert for claims that seem to rely on insufficient evidence or evidence that is highly selective, since either condition may indicate that the author is intentionally concealing information that would damage his or her claim. Pay attention as well to arguments that seem to ignore opposing positions on the issue, since such disregard may indicate an effort to pass off a claim that is weak or widely discredited.

In considering whether claims are invalid because of flawed reasoning we enter the realm of logic, and, in particular, of fallacies, the blanket term for false reasoning of various sorts. The form of flawed reasoning that is open to the most devastating critique is also one of the easiest to spot: contradiction. If a text contains contradictory claims, one of them has to be false. Read further for a description of some common fallacies.

To resolve or critique: Here, critique can follow a three-step procedure. First, identify the claim or argument you believe to be untruthful or unsound; then, if necessary, characterize it as a deliberate evasion or as an unintentional flaw in reasoning. Finally, as the third step, refute the claim by explaining precisely why it is flawed.

Validity Claim 4: Appropriateness

Does the argument draw upon a value system (a coherent set of moral and ethical norms or beliefs) that is not appropriate to the issue?

Even if a text is intelligible, has its facts in order, and avoids false claims, its argument may still reflect a value system that you find inappropriate to the issue at hand. For example, some cultures see dogs as pets, others as livestock; some cultures see cows as livestock, others as sacred animals. In such cases, the arguments on both sides may be intelligible and sincere, yet totally opposed.

The validity claim of appropriateness is thus perhaps the most significant of all, since it underlies the deepest and most intractable types of disagreements and conflicts. Indeed, intractable issues such as abortion tend to be characterized by radically divergent value systems or world views and thus raise the greatest challenge to argumentative resolution.

In considering whether the value system underlying an argument is appropriate or not, you first need to identify the values involved. Sometimes these will be explicitly stated in the text, but frequently the key values are implicit to the argument: the argument *assumes* them without overt articulation. For this reason, it is crucially important when critiquing a text to work backward from what is argued to the world view that must necessarily ground that argument.

For example, in the 1930s German Nazis appealed to quasi-scientific values (now thoroughly discredited) to argue that mental patients should be subject to euthanasia, but their position also assumed certain values—the superman myth, racial superiority, the subservence of the individual to the state—that were much less likely to be openly stated. In critiquing such a position, you would want to analyze both the assumed as well as the explicit values.

To resolve or critique: In some cases you may find it possible to suggest that the value system underlying an argument is genuinely inappropriate to the issue. Your object is then to explain the shortcomings of the inappropriate value system, usually proposing an alternative of your own.

Example of inappropriate value system in argumentation: In *The Hitchhiker's Guide to the Galaxy*, after a colony of humans has accidentally been time-shifted back to the Stone Age, a committee is formed to reinvent the wheel so that civilization may be restarted. Unfortunately, the committee consists of marketing experts who argue for months over what color the wheel should be. Here a critique might maintain that aesthetic values are less appropriate to the issue at hand—the re-establishment of civilization—than the practical objective of producing, as quickly as possible, a disk attached to an axle…no matter what the color.

In critiquing impacted issues (again, such as abortion), where competing value systems underlie arguments, the task becomes more difficult. Here, refutation cannot expect to achieve much, so critique needs to pursue a bridging role looking for common values and trying to arrive at a rational and a mutually agreeable protocol defining the conditions under which one or the other value system should have priority.

The Toulmin Framework for Analyzing Arguments

In his landmark work, *The Uses of Argument*, English philosopher and former USC Professor Stephen Toulmin developed a six-part model of argumentation that has been used as a tool for examining and dissecting persuasive texts. Toulmin's method demanded that reasoning be scrutinized as more than just the line between assertion and evidence. He believed that one also needed to analyze all critical assumptions made to reach an author's ultimate conclusion. Toulmin's six parts of an argument are:

1. **Claim**: an idea that the author is attempting to defend; a claim would include the thesis, or central conclusion of the essay, as well as any ideas offered to help build toward the thesis

2. **Qualifier**: any limitations on the claim intended to clarify its scope

3. **Grounds**: the evidence offered to support the claim

4. **Warrant**: the connection between the claim and grounds; a necessary assumption for explaining why the evidence supports the claim

5. **Backing**: the justification for the warrant, explaining why a given assumption or warrant is valid

6. **Rebuttal**: a counterargument for any of the elements above

Analyzing an Argument Using the Toulmin Method

A *qualified claim* could be as simple as: "Winner of the 2018 Academy Award for Best Picture, Guillermo del Toro's *The Shape of Water* was the greatest film released in 2017." The *qualifier*, "released in 2017," narrows the scope of the thesis. The grounds offered to support the claim is the fact that *The Shape of Water* won Best Picture at the 2018 Academy Awards. These elements are easy to detect as they are almost always explicitly stated.

So if the claim above is clear and the offered grounds are indisputable, why would so many disagree with the statement above? Because agreeing with the claim necessitates that the reader accept the assumption or *warrant* that films that win Best Picture are always the greatest films released in a given year. If one does not agree with the underlying warrant, the claim becomes invalid.

Let's imagine that the author of this thesis has anticipated this objection. A type of *backing* the author could offer to defend it would be pointing out that the Academy of Motion Picture Arts and Sciences is composed of the foremost experts in the craft of filmmaking and are accordingly the most authoritative arbiters of movie greatness.

Still not convinced? No doubt: at least some of the following *rebuttals* come to mind:

- *For the grounds:* Why didn't the author posit more than just one piece of evidence—a Best Picture win—to support the claim? Greatness can be measured in many ways, including critical acclaim, longevity, and box office success. Why limit the criteria so narrowly?
- *For the qualifier:* Did the author consider films released outside of the United States?
- *For the warrant:*
  - Do Academy Awards measure the "greatness" of films? Like all awards, don't they only measure popularity in a given moment among a set cohort?
  - Hasn't hindsight shown that some of the "greatest" films in history lost their bid for Best Picture, including what many film scholars consider to be *the* greatest film of all time, *Citizen Kane*?

- *For the backing*:
  - What are the criteria for admission into the Academy of Motion Picture Arts and Sciences? Is it really a requirement that members be the "foremost experts" in their field?
  - Is the Academy really the most authoritative arbiter of movie greatness? What about film critics and scholars? What about the public audience who pays to see the movies?

The above analysis might seem like much ado about nothing given how obviously problematic the central claim is. But look at how many interesting questions—about the nature of "greatness," about what it means to be an authority in a field—are unearthed from a Toulmin analysis. Imagine how many other interesting questions can be uncovered when tackling more considered, more formidable arguments. The Toulmin framework is meant as a tool. As daunting and unfamiliar as it may be at first glance, it merely codifies many of your own natural argumentative instincts and does so in a way that generates new ways of thinking about a given topic.

When breaking down a persuasive text as a reader, consider the following steps:

1. **Identify the claim.** What is the author trying to say? Claims can be factual in nature (*The Shape of Water* won the 2018 Academy Award for Best Picture); they can make moral, ethical, or aesthetic judgments (*The Shape of Water* was the greatest film of 2017); they can offer opinions on policy (Human beings should be allowed to carry on amorous relationships with Amazonian sea monsters).

2. **Understand the claim's qualifiers and exceptions.** Is the claim presented as an absolute or are there circumstances when the claim does not apply?

3. **Identify the grounds.** Evidence can take the form of facts (like dates, historical events, and statistics), opinions (the testimony of an expert in a field), examples (both real and hypothetical), and even images (like a photograph or a still frame from a video).

4. **Determine any warrants.** What critical assumptions are necessary for an audience to accept that the evidence constitutes valid proof for the argument?

5. **Determine any backing for the warrants.** Has the author presented additional support to assure the audience that the warrants are valid?

6. **Identify and posit rebuttals.** Has the author anticipated resistance to the elements above as well as other perspectives? Can *you* see any counterarguments that the author has failed to include?

The Toulmin framework is also useful when crafting your own arguments. Consider the following road map:

1. **Form a tentative claim.** If Toulmin teaches us anything, it's that even beliefs that border on certainty (perhaps *especially* beliefs that border on certainty) need to be examined and pressed.

2. **Determine what kinds of grounds or support you need to make your claim.** Research facts and authorities on the subject; craft or locate examples to illuminate your argument.

3. **Determine what warrants you've relied on to connect your claim and grounds.** Do you actually believe in the assumptions you've made? Do you believe that your audience will also agree?

4. **Provide any necessary backing to support your warrants.** What kind of reasoning will ensure that your audience accepts the assumptions underlying your analysis?

5. **Consider rebuttals and craft counterarguments for what you believe to be the most salient weaknesses in your argument.** Considering weaknesses early can help ensure a sturdy, tightly written argument.

6. **Qualify your claim.** Once you've done all of the above and determined the proper strength and scope of your tentative claim, you can now qualify that claim to make it is as precise as possible.

One final note: Toulmin himself warned against prescribing to any idea dogmatically, conceding that the Toulmin framework wasn't equally suited to all types of argumentation in all fields. Again, this framework is a tool, one of many in this course book, but one that you should consider, especially if you're having trouble generating ideas from an uninspiring subject or a flawed argument you are tasked with critiquing. Most reasoning is layered, and it is useful for any reader or author to be able to cull those layers and analyze them separately to understand the durability of the argument as a whole. While the effort might seem like analytical overkill, remember Toulmin's Law of Composition: "The effort the writer does not put into writing, the reader has to put into reading."

Logical Fallacies

While there are many ways to impede the analysis of a complex issue, some of the most obstructive and detrimental are collectively referred to as **logical fallacies**. Think of logical fallacies as a sort of analytical or argumentative cheating: they are deceptive and they weaken rather than strengthen our ability to explore and understand issues. It is therefore important to be able to identify and characterize logical fallacies, both so that we will avoid allowing them to slip into our own analysis or argument, and so that we can recognize and refute them when employed by others. Here are some common fallacies to be alert for:

***Ad Hominem* Attacks**: Those whose own position is weak often choose to attack their opponent's character rather than his or her arguments. These *ad hominem* tactics include the fallacies of **name-calling** and **poisoning the well** (attempting to bias an audience so they will not listen to an opponent's claims). By directing attention away from ideas and evidence and toward personalities, *ad hominem* attacks blur our understanding of the issue being discussed. Unless personal information has direct rather than peripheral relevance to the argument, it should not be introduced. Of course, there may be reasonable disagreement as to when personal information is directly relevant. For instance, are the details of a politician's personal life unrelated to his or her job performance and thus irrelevant, or indicative of that person's fundamental character and thus highly relevant?

Bandwagon Appeal: This fallacy relies on popularity rather than reasoning: "Everyone else is downloading music without paying for it, so you should, too." Common in advertising ("Buy Chocolate-Frosted Sugar Bombs, the most popular cereal in America!"), the bandwagon appeal or **appeal to common practice** was also used by many of us when we were children: "But all my friends get to stay up 'til eleven!" The reasoning is flawed because common practice does not necessarily justify the appropriateness of a particular action.

Begging the Question: A form of circular reasoning in which a claim is restated, usually in different words, as support for itself: "I believe we will find weapons of mass destruction because I am confident they are there." The fundamental terms here might be reversed with very little difference in meaning: "I believe because I am confident; I am confident because I believe." Such circularity precludes the development of any chain of reasoning whereby explanations and evidence are adduced in *support* of the main claim, and this in turn prevents any authentic analysis of the issue.

Equivocation: A linguistic slight-of-hand whereby the key term in an argument is employed in an ambiguous manner that reflects two or more different meanings: "A democrat is a person who is committed to democratic principles, and especially to the doctrine of government by the people; Rosemary, a Republican, is an outspoken opponent of Democrats and of their principles; therefore, Rosemary is an opponent of government by the people." Here the equivocation (Latin: *equi* [equal] + *vox* [voice]) would suggest that opposing Democrats (members of a particular political party) is the same thing as opposing democrats (proponents of democratic forms of government), an argument that is plainly fallacious but that may sound valid because of the equivocal use of *democrat* and *Democrat*.

False Authority: This fallacy bases its appeal on an authority figure who lacks competence in the field under consideration. False authority is a particularly dangerous form of fallacious reasoning in an era that is enthralled with celebrity, and any number of examples of this fallacy may be found in contemporary advertisements and popular journals.

False Dichotomy: Almost by definition, complex arguments place a range of options and ideas into consideration. Those who make use of the fallacy of false dichotomy try to maintain that the issue permits only two options, the one they favor (presented in glowing terms) and a worst-case representative of the opposing side (usually set up as a **straw-person argument**). Example: "The United States must either wage war on terrorism until every terrorist has been eliminated or sit back and allow terrorists to destroy the United States." In coercively restricting the range of potential responses, false dichotomies sharply limit our ability to explore and understand problems.

Hasty Generalization: A hasty generalization makes a broad claim on the basis of narrow evidence, and sometimes on the basis of only one or two examples: "While in prison, this man was part of a new program to prepare convicts for life on the outside. The day after he was released from prison, he robbed a gas station at gunpoint. Obviously, such reform programs are a failure and funding for them should be withdrawn." There is no clear formula for what constitutes "sufficient" evidence, but significant claims require significant support, and here only one case is mentioned. If the reform program really is a failure, similar examples of recidivism ought to be abundant, and enough of them—a statistically relevant sample—must be presented in order to provide plausible support for the proposed elimination of the program. Absent of such support, the proposal cannot be considered valid.

Non sequitur: "It does not follow." While almost any fallacy may be said to involve conclusions that don't follow from the reasoning provided, a *non sequitur* is distinguished by reasoning or evidence that is exceptionally irrelevant to the claim being made: "Cats are evil because they're too fast." On this logic, deer and falcons would apparently be even more evil than felines.

Oversimplification: An argument in which complex causal relationships are reduced or ignored in favor of a simple claim that fails to address significant dimensions of the issue: "The only way to end crime is to eliminate poverty." While poverty is undoubtedly an important factor in criminal behavior, it is plainly not the *only* factor, since individuals who are not poor commit many crimes. Eliminating poverty is thus not the (sole) way to end crime.

Post Hoc, Ergo Propter Hoc: "After this, therefore because of this." The *post hoc* fallacy (as it is usually called) confuses chronology with causation, asserting that because one event happened *after* another, it must have been caused *by* the earlier event. Example: "After President Bush was elected, the economy took a dive. Therefore, Bush must be responsible for the recession." This assertion ignores the possibility that the economy may have been headed for a recession before President Bush was elected, and it provides no explanation as to how the Bush administration's policies might be responsible for the economic downturn. Quick and simple claims of this sort discourage one from carefully examining the overall situation, looking for other contributing factors and for genuine chains of causation. As H. L. Mencken wrote, "For every complex problem, there is a simple solution. And it is wrong."

Red Herring: This fallacy is named for a technique supposedly once used by criminals as an aid in escaping the scene of a crime. By dragging a fish across their tracks, the criminals were able to mislead pursuing bloodhounds, which would follow the stronger scent of the red (i.e., rotten) herring. In argumentation, the red herring fallacy consists of introducing an irrelevant but sensational issue in order to divert the argument from its proper focus. Such diversions make it very difficult to advance understanding of the real issue. The red herring fallacy will also weaken the organization of an argument, as the discussion will quite literally veer away from the issue at hand.

Slippery Slope: This is a very common type of fallacy in debates on contentious social issues. The fallacy implies that a small step in a certain direction, in personal choice or social policy, will inevitably lead one down a slippery slope toward ruin and disaster. Example: "If reality television is not prohibited, it will cause viewers to lose all ability to distinguish between the real and the unreal, and this will ultimately result in their not being able to think at all." If such consequences are truly imminent, their inevitability needs to be fully explained (with each step thoroughly analyzed and demonstrated); responsible argumentation provides reasons, not simply claims or predictions.

Stirring Symbols: Sometimes also referred to as **flag waving**, this fallacy uses powerful symbols to appeal to our emotions instead of our reason, and is often on display in election years. For example, at some point during a senatorial campaign, a candidate may appear on television engaged in a heartfelt talk with an American farmer. Her opponent may have spent the morning reading stories to preschool children. Through such photo opportunities, politicians attempt to persuade voters by associating themselves with moving cultural symbols: the farmer, the child, the schoolhouse, or the American flag. Though emotionally affecting and visually stirring, such appeals do not offer any substantive evidence that the candidates deserve our votes, and they do nothing to advance our understanding of genuine issues.

Straw-Person Arguments: A straw-person argument is actually an invalid form of *counter*argument: one sets up an exaggerated, simplified, or perhaps even falsified version of the opposing position and then "refutes" it with claims that ignore the opponent's actual reasoning. "Winning" a straw-person argument is thus as easy as knocking over a scarecrow and may sometimes even give the illusion of argumentative competence, but such tactics contribute little to our understanding of the issues involved in any dispute. For example, in an exchange between Bishop Wilberforce and Thomas Huxley in 1860 over the issue of evolutionary theory, Bishop Wilberforce apparently felt he might be able to score debating points when he asked Huxley whether it was from his grandmother's side or his grandfather's that he claimed descent from a monkey. This deliberately simplistic distortion of Huxley's position backfired on Wilberforce, causing many in the audience actually to gain sympathy for Huxley's side of the argument, perhaps because the bishop's straw-person representation of Huxley's views also smacked of an *ad hominem* attack. The straw-person fallacy reverses the principle of fairly restating opposing positions; as mentioned above, it is both more honest and more intelligent to enunciate opposing viewpoints in language that their adherents would approve.

Argumentation

Many forms of writing—reports, proposals, essays, surveys, articles, books—are important within the various discourse communities that constitute the university, but most of these forms have one thing in common: a need for careful analysis and argumentation. The major goals of the university—research, criticism, and teaching—all depend not simply on careful study, but also on a willingness to convince others with arguments justifying our analysis of a situation and, in turn, on an equal willingness to open ourselves to the possibility of being convinced by their arguments and analysis. Because this sort of dialogic interchange is not only characteristic of, but also crucial to the work of the university, academic analysis and argumentation are indispensable skills, and thus key themes of Writing 150.

For this reason, it is important to recognize that within an academic context the term argument does not mean quite what it does in everyday life. In common usage, an argument usually implies an adversarial relationship between two or more people. These kinds of adversarial arguments may involve one side trying to prove the other side wrong or, less confrontationally, an attempt by one side to negotiate a compromise with the other. In either case, what is at stake is primarily a matter of power, a question of which side will dominate or what balance of power can be negotiated.

While everyone needs to be able to participate occasionally in adversarial forms of argumentation, many of the tactics and strategies used in adversarial arguments are inappropriate when employed in academic discourse. Academic analysis and argumentation have purposes that differ in important respects from those of adversarial argument. Even though academic arguments are often conducted in a sharp and vigorous manner, their function is not to establish power but rather to achieve reasoned understanding and uncoerced assent. What finally matters in this form of argumentation is not whose position is shown to be stronger or weaker, but the quality of the argument itself, whether it advances or impedes our pursuit of knowledge and truth, whether it helps us to analyze a situation critically and to act with integrity. The outcome of such argumentation therefore depends not upon the strength of any one argumentative position but upon the willingness of all participants to address the issue in a spirit of intellectual honesty and goodwill.

This means, in turn, that those who engage in academic discourse need to address the complexities of the issue under consideration, to think carefully not only about their own ideas and arguments, but also about those advanced by others. Each participant in academic discourse has a responsibility to advance the position he or she genuinely believes to be true and to argue his or her case fairly but forcefully. But the final responsibility of *all* participants must be toward what the German philosopher Jurgen Habermas has called "the unforced force of the better argument." This "better argument" can only be attained in an analytical and argumentative environment that encourages the complex interplay of numerous voices and positions.

Argumentation from a Rhetorical Perspective

The approach to analysis and argumentation described above derives from the long tradition of rhetoric that began in Athens nearly 2,500 years ago. As the first academic subject ever to be formally taught, and as a particularly contentious field, rhetoric has accumulated a large and diverse collection of theories and principles: any strong claim as to the nature of rhetoric can usually be contradicted by citing an authority who maintains the opposite position. Nonetheless, it is useful to keep in mind two general points about the rhetorical perspective on argumentation.

This perspective recognizes, first of all, that humans can know few things with certainty and that argumentation is thus primarily a means of dealing with conditions of **uncertainty**. Most human problems—whether they are social, ethical, or political—fall outside the domain of certainty; they cannot be resolved solely through logic or calculation or scientific procedure. Even when we can claim to know something with certainty—for example, that global temperatures appear to be rising—we are still faced with resultant issues that are highly uncertain and that cannot be resolved simply by reading thermometers: Why are temperatures rising? Is the rise reflective of a recurrent natural cycle or of a disruption of that cycle through human activity? Can the temperature change be reversed? If so, should it be? If actions are to be taken, what should they be and how should they be enforced? What countries or industries should bear the cost of any remedial action?

Questions such as these are matters of practical reasoning and thus of rhetoric. While practical reasoning makes whatever use it can of logic and science, its purpose is entirely different. Rather than attempting to achieve certainty, practical reasoning tries instead to identify the best course of action or the best analysis of a situation, always under conditions that make certainty or precise calculation impossible. Practical reasoning is central to rhetoric because rhetoric also concerns itself with choosing the best course of action when decisions must be made in the absence of certainty.

In recognizing limitations concerning what can be definitively known, the rhetorical perspective entails a second important principle of argumentation: in the absence of certainty, it becomes crucial to be **open-minded** in approaching any argumentative issue. Protagoras, the first of the sophistic rhetoricians, reflected this concern in his development of the concept of "antilogic," the careful examination of arguments on both sides of a dispute. Cicero, the greatest orator and rhetorician of the Roman republic, was even more emphatic in this regard. Central to Ciceronian rhetorical theory is the doctrine of *in utramque partem*, the idea that in approaching an argumentative situation the rhetor (the speaker or writer) should prepare to argue either side of the dispute or any relevant position within the issue. On this view, argumentation remains a means of persuasion, but on a deeper level it also serves as a mode of understanding: to convince others, we have to be familiar not only with our own views and interests, but with theirs.

Counterargument

From the rhetorical perspective, counterargument is as significant as argument itself. Properly considered, counterargument should be thought of not as an element that may be introduced only at certain places within an argument—"My counterargument paragraph comes right after the introduction,"—but rather as a fundamental dimension of argumentation itself, one that should inform *every* paragraph within an argument. As Protagoras and Cicero both understood, disputed issues become issues because reasonable people disagree about them, so that valid points can be raised on all sides of any genuine issue. To argue any point effectively, therefore, one must be able to engage the arguments that a fair-minded reader knows would be raised by the opposing side.

Unfortunately, counterargument often takes one of two tacks—an *ad hominem* approach in which the person and character of one's opponent rather than his or her arguments are attacked, or a straw-person perspective in which opposing arguments are misrepresented, distorted, or simplified so that they can be easily dismissed.

When seriously implemented, counterargument reveals weaknesses in one's proposals or the reasons behind them. This is a devil's advocate stance in which a writer meticulously searches for gaps in logic that should be shored up. Second, an open discussion of opposing positions reflects intellectual honesty. Again, since so few genuine controversies can be separated easily into one right and several wrong camps, it is unlikely that any one party can claim sole possession of the truth. The honest debater will acknowledge the other side of an argument and concede that his or her opponents may have something of value to add to the discussion.

How, then, does one handle competing claims in an academic context? By adopting the perspective of *in utramque partem* ("and on the other hand…") one does not belittle opposing arguments but rather engages them, accepting those parts of them that may hold truth and denoting where one departs from them. For example, an advocate of the recall process in politics may concede that the cost of the process is high, yet still contend that the recall provision provides a means by which democracy remains vibrant. From the opposite perspective, an opponent of the recall process may grant that an official has made mistakes in office, yet still argue that these are insufficient to justify the time, expense, and distraction that a recall election necessitates. This approach is a more subtle and sophisticated form of argumentation that avoids reductionism but reflects evenhandedness.

By employing this method, one may find that opposing positions offer valid claims that cannot conscientiously be swept aside. In that instance, here are two ways to handle them:

Concession: This rhetorical move is the recognition of points that contradict one's own argument. If exceptions to one's argument exist, far better to concede them oneself than to have them trumpeted by one's opponents. Have faith that a reasonable audience will appreciate honest engagement. Concession may take the form of granting an exception as simply that, an *exception* that doesn't disprove the preponderance of evidence that still remains on one's own side of the argument.

As an example, one could reject just war theory, the *ad jus bellum* of medieval philosophers, as impractical in our time while still conceding that evil in the world remains very real. In contrast, a pragmatist acknowledges that both individuals and states are quite capable of visiting great harm on others but may still insist that recourse to war is not the best way of dealing with this situation. Sometimes a concession is just another way of noting that what is being conceded is no longer relevant to the issue in dispute.

Qualification: This element involves more than conceding a single point or "exception to the rule" on the part of an opponent's arguments. Qualification may actually demonstrate how complex some issues are and how they admit neither a single cause nor remedy.

Suppose, for example, that one wishes to argue that poverty is a multifaceted problem with many causes and that, in addressing this problem, one or more facets have been neglected. Suppose further that one's opponent has taken a different stance by suggesting that a single cause, perhaps racism, is the most crucial factor leading to poverty. Here one could effectively qualify one's position by noting that racism is indeed a significant contributor to poverty while still maintaining that other causes are also at work, and that they must be addressed, as well.

Concession and qualification are essential tools supporting academic argument and counterargument. Each requires that one honestly and fairly explore opponents' positions and discerns those that have merit while rejecting those that do not.

Refutation: Neither concession nor qualification requires one to abandon refutation, however. In engaging opposing arguments, one must refute those points that have no validity, provided one fully explains why.

Protocols for refutation vary. One may take on an opponent's theses one-by-one, as they are presented in his or her argument, noting and countering them in sequence and in paragraph form. Or one may arrange them in a hierarchy of importance, taking on the most crucial ones first or last. Or, in yet another variation, one may list them en masse and then refute them in the same fashion.

Audience Awareness

A Traditional Approach: Aristotle

Aristotle conceived the purpose of rhetoric to be to *persuade* the audience, and he identified three types of "proofs" by which such persuasion might be achieved: through appeals to *logos,* to *ethos,* and to *pathos.*

Logos involves reasoning about the substance of the issue under consideration;

Ethos involves arguments derived from the character of the *rhetor*—the speaker or writer;

Pathos involves arguments intended to stir the emotions of the audience.

These three methods of argumentative appeal constitute what is sometimes referred to as the *rhetorical triangle,* and they provide a handy means of analyzing the qualities of many sorts of arguments. Wayne Booth, the late American literary critic, speaks of "the rhetorical stance," an appropriate balance of logical, ethical, and pathetic appeals. Some arguments give nearly equal weight to each of these three different types of appeals, but other arguments, especially those taking place within more specialized discursive circumstances, may require giving greater weight to one of the appeals and relatively less to the other two. In a scientific or scholarly paper, for instance, one usually places greatest emphasis on *logos,* on carefully analyzing and arguing the facts and theories pertinent to the issue at hand. Yet even in this context, it is vitally important to present one's argument in a manner that doesn't undermine one's credibility (*ethos*) and that recognizes and respects the values of the audience or discourse community (*pathos*). Thus, to continue the example, even if the *logos* of an academic essay is fairly solid, lapses in grammar or style or errors in the citation of sources are likely to be read against the *ethos* of the writer and therefore weaken the overall strength of the argument.

Moderation is key to achieving a balanced rhetorical stance, and Booth described three immoderate or exaggerated stances that occur with some frequency. One is the pedant's stance, a dry, lifeless commitment to logic and substance that makes no attempt to connect with the audience and that is bereft of any sense of personal voice or tone. Another is the advertiser's stance, which is so wholly committed to currying favor with the audience that it distorts or falsifies the subject of discussion. And the third is the entertainer's stance, one that uses the issue primarily as a stage from which to deliver a self-centered display of ego and empty cleverness to an adoring audience. If you find your argument drifting in any of these directions, change course.

Two Modern Approaches: Burke and Rogers

Burkean Identification

The American literary critic and intellectual Kenneth Burke extended the traditional Aristotelian understanding of rhetoric as a means of persuasion by associating that concept with the idea of "identification." Burke suggested that successful persuasion depends upon uncovering some sort of shared identity between the parties disputing an issue. In order to persuade another person, one must be able to locate common ground, some form of mutual identification in terms of values or interests.

It follows from this perspective that argumentation involves an effort not to manipulate but to understand those with whom we dispute an issue. While argumentation is often spoken of in terms of adversarial metaphors—"winning a debate" or "scoring points"—Burke saw language and rhetoric as necessary precisely because they constitute our best means of overcoming the division and distanciation that characterize much of human existence.

In developing an argumentative position, therefore, one should always consider not only where one differs from those on the other side, but also where one shares values, beliefs, or commitments with them. Arguments that draw upon both the divergent and the mutual, relating them together, are likely to be more persuasive and more productive than those that focus solely on differences.

Rogerian Redirection

Carl Rogers was a psychologist who devised a communication protocol that has significant implications for argumentation. In counseling sessions involving two or more people, Rogers made it a rule that before one party could reply to the claim of another, he or she first had to restate that claim *in words that were acceptable to the other person*. This tactic helps to keep argumentative discourse on track by disallowing "straw-person" misrepresentations and by providing frequent opportunities to redirect the argument should it begin to drift away from the issue.

Roger's procedure, developed in the context of oral discourse, stands as an excellent principle for written argumentation as well. If you want your argument to be well received, you should avoid misstating the opposing position and catch yourself whenever you start to stray from the issue at hand. One way to do this is to imagine your argument as an oral debate, and to check each point you make to be sure that it is directly relevant to your main line of argument and does not misrepresent points raised in opposition to your own. By the same token, it is both an appropriate and effective method of rebuttal to point out places in an opponent's argument where similar care has not been taken in reproducing your position.

Example: Applying Burke and Rogers

Imagine the case of a sixteen-year-old who is arguing with his or her parents for a later curfew. Here is how the two different approaches might work.

Burkean Argument: I know we're all working toward the same goal here. I've taken on a lot of responsibility with a part-time job and a community service project, and I believe that it is important for me to maintain an active social life to balance the other commitments I'm responsible for. I agree with you that I'm not ready for all night or even early morning curfew. I don't want to face the pressure of having that kind of temptation. But since many of the important events this school year end after 10:00, and I have always been careful to respect my curfew so far, I believe that a curfew of midnight would be appropriate at my age.

Rogerian Argument: Mom, Dad. I understand your point of view. You are worried that a later curfew will affect my grades and encourage me to become involved in activities that could get me into trouble. We have heard about kids my age who drank while out late and tried to drive home, or let another kid who had been drinking drive. You're also worried that my grades might suffer if I am out late frequently. That's why I propose that we work gradually toward raising my curfew. We can work out a contract specifying what goals and requirements I need to meet for each step so that I can prove I can be trusted with a later return time.

Invention

The most important function of prewriting is invention, the development of ideas and material to use in a paper. While the term implies the creation of something entirely new, invention is more often a process of recollection and reflection. The invention process usually starts by recalling fairly familiar information—the first things that spring to mind when thinking about the topic. The key step in invention, however, is to *move beyond your initial ideas*, and that is what you should seek to do as you reflect upon your initial ideas.

Appropriation of Writing Task

When you receive a writing assignment, your first job, even before you start sketching out ideas, is to make sure that you thoroughly understand what the assignment calls for. Before you begin to write, you want to make the writing task your own—to appropriate it—so that you can engage the issue fully and thus offer a more creative and insightful response.

In appropriating a writing task, begin with the prompt itself, underlining or otherwise identifying the key terms that most fundamentally constitute the issue it raises. For example, the prompt for a writing section used in the thematic group "Human Values and Belief Systems" might ask, "What are the most important ethical consequences of materialism?" The key terms here are *materialism* and *ethical consequences*, and any effective response to this question will have to focus on these concepts from the opening paragraph to the conclusion. You may wish to record the key concepts as the basis of a cluster or brainstorming list.

Once you have a sense of the key terms of the writing prompt, go back and read through the entire assignment sheet, looking for anything that extends or qualifies the writing task or that relates to any of the key terms you have identified. In the Writing Program, assignments typically include a statement of rhetorical purpose (the writing skills that the assignment is designed to have you practice), a list of relevant readings, a discussion of the writing topic, an explicit statement of the issue or writing task, and a list of ancillary suggestions or requirements, including due dates. Except (perhaps) for the statement of rhetorical purpose, each of these sections is likely to include information pertinent to a full understanding of the writing task. Pay particular attention to ancillary requirements and to whatever hints or suggestions your instructor may have included, but underline anything that seems to relate to the issue, and record these potential relationships on your cluster or brainstorming list. In the sample assignment that follows, a number of relevant "starting points" have been underlined to demonstrate how much information may be obtained from the assignment sheet itself. Terms to consider in their relationship to the writing task have been underlined <u>once</u>, while ancillary requirements have been underlined <u>twice</u>.

Naturally, if you have any questions about what an assignment calls for or about the meaning or significance of any terms or concepts on the assignment sheet, be sure to ask such questions in class. You will often discover that several of your classmates may share your puzzlement, and instructors welcome the opportunity such questions provide to clarify the assignment so that all students can get off to a good start.

The cluster or brainstorming list you create in analyzing the assignment sheet makes an excellent jumping-off point from which to begin your writing process, and can also serve as a checklist to review against your developing drafts to make sure you have addressed all dimensions of the writing task. See below for a sample brainstorming list analyzing an assignment sheet.

Example: Appropriating the Writing Task

Section 99999   Assignment # 1   Writing 150

The Ethical Implicature of Materialism   Fall 2018

Purpose

Much of our work with this first assignment will involve prewriting. We will begin developing a set of invention skills, concentrating here on the inscriptive techniques of clustering and listing and on two heuristic techniques, one (the fact/idea list) representing inferential invention and another derived from the classical topoi. We will also work on matters of arrangement, practicing the use of points-to-make lists and rough plans and engaging in an initial approach to thesis development. Finally, we will begin working on matters of revision and style.

Readings

Excerpt from William Leach's _Land of Desire: Merchants, Power, and the Rise of a New American Culture_.

Writing 150 Course Book: pp. xv–xviii (An overview of the Writing Process, The Process of Writing, How to Use This Book), pp. 22–35 (Heuristics: Techniques for Developing Ideas, Points-to-Make Lists, Developing a Provisional Thesis Idea)

Premise

As the excerpt from _Land of Desire_ makes clear, over the course of the last century America has become a "consumer culture" in which materialism—the desire for wealth and possessions—plays an exceptionally large role. Given the importance of materialism within almost every dimension of American culture, it is equally evident that materialism must have a significant ethical implicature; that is to say, materialism by its very presence must condition how we understand the moral and ethical values that constitute "the good life." But in what manner? While it is not difficult to think of ways in which materialism could have negative ethical repercussions, it is also possible to conceive of materialism as resulting in positive ethical consequences. This assignment is intended to provide you with an opportunity to explore these questions for yourself.

Writing Task

Reflect upon the values that you defined as ethically significant in your diagnostic essay and carefully review the relationships between materialism and ethics that you uncovered in completing the prewriting activities for this assignment. Then respond to the following writing prompt:

In your view, what are the most important ethical consequences of materialism?

In planning and writing your essay, please keep the following ancillary requirements in mind:

> in the context of this assignment, the term ethical consequences should be taken in its common usage to include not only ethical questions (matters pertaining to the nature of the good life) but moral questions (matters of right and wrong) as well;

> in your analysis, be sure to include consideration of both positive and negative ethical consequences, making clear whether you think the negative ethical consequences of materialism outweigh its positive consequences, and why;

> avoid "listing": make sure you integrate your analysis by means of a suitable thesis.

Due Dates

Rough plan due in conference Wednesday, September 5.

Final draft (5–6 pages) due Friday, September 14. With your final draft, please submit all notes and prewriting materials, using a twin-pocketed folder for this purpose.

Brainstorming Questions and Notes

Derived from Assignment Sheet

> How is desire related to materialism and its ethical consequences?

> How does power relate to the same?

> How are materialism and its ethical consequences related to the rise (or decline) of American culture?

> How is consumer culture involved in the ethical consequences of materialism?

> How does materialism condition ethical and moral values? How does it affect "the good life?"

> What are the negative ethical repercussions of materialism? What are positive repercussions?

> Note: Review values defined as ethically significant in diagnostic essay.

> Note: Review prewriting materials.

> Note: Use "ethical consequences" in its common usage (the good life and matters of right and wrong).

> Note: Consider both negative and positive ethical consequences of materialism.

> Note: Avoid listing; integrate argument with strong thesis.

Heuristics: Techniques for Developing Ideas

Heuristics are a kind of catalyst to the invention process, techniques that may be applied to a topic to generate a more extensive set of relationships and ideas. General heuristics may be applied successfully to any topic, but you should also make it a habit to develop specialized heuristics suitable to the particular discipline or subject area in which you are working. To do so, simply make a list or cluster of key concepts (what Kenneth Burke called "god terms") of that field and then apply these during your prewriting to ensure that you reflect upon as many potential relationships and connections as possible. Lists or clusters of god terms also constitute an excellent study method, since they should capture most of what is essential about the field they describe.

Fact/Idea Lists

Often it's easier to develop ideas indirectly—by going from concrete "facts" to abstract "ideas"—than by trying to come up with ideas directly. This type of heuristic is useful because it can be applied to almost any topic or issue; moreover, because this heuristic automatically links concepts with factual evidence, it helps you identify ideas that have a good deal of support associated with them.

To create a fact/idea list, write your topic or issue at the top of a sheet of paper and draw a vertical line beneath it, dividing the page into two columns. Label the column on the left "Facts," and that on the right, "Ideas." Then simply start thinking about the assignment and recording information in the proper column. (You will probably have many more items in the "Facts" column than in the one for "Ideas.") After you have most of the "Facts" column filled up, begin to make connections between the columns. What ideas—concepts, claims, or questions—do you associate with the various facts in the left column? Record these abstractions in the "Ideas" column, drawing a line to indicate the connection if the items aren't side-by-side. Do the same thing with ideas in the right column: ask whether they can be connected with any of the facts already recorded, or whether they cause one to envision new details. In doing so, you will begin to get a sense of those ideas for which you seem to have a great deal of supporting material, as well as those for which you don't.

Once this process is completed, spend a little more time reflecting on the list. What are the most interesting ideas and connections? Which items in the "Ideas" column are linked to abundant supporting material in the "Facts" column, and which are not? What ideas are "groupable," related to one another in some way, and which seem unrelated or isolated? In doing so, keep in mind an important point: while pondering facts is often the best way to discover ideas, the structure of an essay will arise not out of the "Facts" side of the list but rather out of the concepts and abstractions in the "Ideas" column. When you begin sketching out a rough plan for your paper, you will therefore draw upon the "Ideas" column.

Sample Fact/Idea List

The following fact/idea list exemplifies some initial responses that might arise in analyzing the follow prompt from a Writing 150 section in the Technology and Social Change thematic:

Select a contemporary "everyday technology" which, in your view, embodies beliefs and values that can be associated with a particular outlook or worldview. Then respond to the following writing prompt:

How do the values and assumptions embodied in this "naturalized" technology reveal or construct that worldview?

Everyday technology selected: digital media

FACT	IDEA
1. Child less than two years old, tapping pictures in a book, trying to find a hyperlink.	1a. Perhaps implies a "jumpy" view of the world, one in which the expectation is to hop from one bit of information to the next, without dwelling too long or reflecting too deeply. 1b. Also suggests the dominance of electronic literacy/media: child can't yet read, but knows one image should lead to another. 1c. Possible points-to-make: digital media are almost addictive—"Give me my iPad fix or I'll start screaming." Like narcotics: more sensation than substantive change.
2. Selfies	2. Encourages or reflects a kind of narcissism.
3. Social media	3. Some important uses, but what, in the main, characterizes social media? Faux celebrity culture? Self-promotional; advertising for self. Desperate need for followers or friends; strange new form of "individualism."
4. The cell phone "nod," head bent, hand holding phone.	4a. Digital media can be almost self-enclosing; alienating. Train platforms with everyone on their own little island, few conversing. 4b. Attention directed not outward, not toward immediate context, and yet not really inward either.
5a. Parents at soccer match, on their cell phones instead of watching their children compete.	5a. Digital media are said to bring us closer, but it doesn't always work that way.
5b. Family in den, one member looking at TV, one texting, one playing computer game on phone, one listening to music.	5b. Huge potential for distraction from values that are less glitzy but more significant.
6. The 2012 web campaign to arrest Joseph Kony.	6. Went viral, got lots of attention through emotional appeals, but not much action; some claim it shifted attention from more significant problems.

Topoi

The *topoi* is a rhetorical concept that dates back to classical Greece, where it was used as an invention tool in developing arguments. The word *topoi* has the English cognate of "topics," although the original Greek meaning was more closely defined as "places." While "topics" and "places" might not immediately seem closely related, the terms speak to a visuospatial theory of argument and persuasion that continued to develop through early Greek and Roman rhetorical systems. It may prove useful to think of topoi as the place from which we begin to make an argument and the "places" that argument might choose to examine as the essay further develops.

Topoi can be classified as either specific or common, the prior being related to a specific discipline or field of the knowledge and the latter to a broader range of knowledge and argument. The common topoi are an especially productive tool for **invention** because they can be tailored to fit a wide range of arguments. Many topoi exist, so what follows is a selection of some popular topoi and how they can be used to explore ideas for a writing prompt.

For the purposes of WRIT 150, we can consider topoi as a set of rhetorical categories that provide a heuristic first to ask questions about a selected topic and then to produce claims related to that initial questioning. The following categories of topoi and their accompanying questions can be a starting point to exploring a subject, but they are by no means exhaustive. As you approach the prompt through these topoi, consider additional questions that might further allow you to analyze your topic.

The following six topoi represent categories of consideration that help generate ideas for an essay and lead to argumentative claims about a particular topic. These topoi are popular because they are especially helpful for inventing arguments, but you may find it more helpful to develop your own categories of questioning to help generate future arguments. The questions in the table demonstrate just a few of the questions from each category that you might ask as you develop your own argument through topoi. Remember that the more specific you can be in your questions and claims, the more focused and effective your argument can become.

DEFINITION	COMPARISON AND CONTRAST
How is the term/concept of x defined? What are the connotations of x? How have the definitions of x shifted over time? What parts (y, z, etc.) make up x? What are similar terms/concepts to x?	What are the parts of x and how do they relate to each other? How are the parts of x different? How does x relate to another term/concept?

ORIGINS AND CONSEQUENCES	REASONS FOR AND AGAINST
What are the means of x and to what end? What is the origin of x? What are the consequences of x? What comes before/after x?	What are the reasons someone might be in favor of x? What are the reasons against x? In what ways might someone have mixed opinions about x? In what ways can x be considered beyond the binary of either/or?

POSSIBILITY	VALUES
What is possible as a result of x? What makes x possible? What makes x more or less possible? What factors contribute to the likelihood of x occurring?	What are the ethical/moral values that affect opinions of x? What are the practical implications of x and how do those influence how the problem is valued? How do the values of a particular society shape the consideration of x? How do political systems/beliefs influence x? How do spiritual/metaphysical values influence x?

The following material demonstrates a two-step procedure whereby topoi are first used to generate questions (Step 1), which are then converted into potential claims (Step 2).

Step 1: Generating Questions

The following exercise demonstrates how the topoi can be used to generate topic-specific questions in response to a prompt used in a WRIT 150 section within a thematic pertaining to health and healing.

Does substance abuse represent a legitimate form of social deviance?

DEFINITION: *Investigate the definition of important terms related to the subject.*

> How do we define substance abuse?

> How do we define social deviance?

> What do we mean by "legitimate form"?

> How has the term "social deviance" changed over time? What might that change signify for the purposes of this argument?

> What parts can substance abuse be divided into? How does the categorization of different substances affect whether we view them as causing substance abuse?

> What other words have a similar meaning to substance abuse/social deviance?

COMPARISON AND CONTRAST: *Question the ways in which the subject is similar to or different from other issues or ideas.*

> What substances comprise our consideration of "substance abuse"? How are those substances similar to one another? How are they different?

> Are certain substances "worse" in regards to social deviance? Why?

> What practices comprise our consideration of "social deviance"? How are those forms of deviancy related to substance abuse? How are they different?

> Is it possible to abuse certain substances but not be socially deviant? How so?

> What other factors may influence our understanding and attitudes toward substance abuse? How do those compare to other forms of social deviancy?

ORIGINS AND CONSEQUENCES: *Consider the relationship between means and ends; origins of the issue; and consequences of certain outcomes.*

> Substance abuse is a means to what possible ends? Which of those ends are deviant? Which are not? Why?

> What causes substance abuse?

> What comes before substance abuse?

> What are the individual consequences of substance abuse?

> What are the social consequences of substance abuse?

> What comes before social deviancy?

> What results from social deviancy?

> What sort of long-term changes or effects will substance abuse lead to?

REASONS FOR AND AGAINST: *Consider the reasons by which one might agree or disagree with the subject, its premises, and its conclusions.*

> Is substance abuse the cause of social deviancy? In what ways is social deviancy not caused by substance abuse?

> Is the classification of substance abuse as social deviancy fair?

> Why would one argue in favor of the idea that substance abuse represents a legitimate form of social deviancy? What factors might influence them to make that argument?

> Why would one argue against this premise?

> Are there distinctions among different types or practices of substance abuse that are more or less problematic? Why?

POSSIBILITY: *Consider the possible outcomes of this issue/argument.*

> Is it possible to resolve the issue of substance abuse in society? If yes, how? If no, why not?

> What would it take to address the issue of substance abuse in America right now?

> What circumstances make substance abuse possible?

> If substance abuse were addressed, what other issues of social deviancy would be equally or more problematic?

> What would prevent social deviancy from happening even if one were to engage in substance abuse?

> What structures could prevent this issue in the future?

VALUES: *Consider the issue in terms of different values, including ethical/moral, practical, social, political, and spiritual/metaphysical.*

> In what ways are definitions of deviance and perspectives on substance abuse determined or informed by our **ethical/moral** standards or accepted social norms?

> What **practical** implications or consequences of substance abuse can you identify? Do some practical implications outweigh others in terms of their significance or applicability to the abuser? To their family? To society in general?

> Many argue that society ultimately bears the burden of substance abuse. How is **society** implicated in definitions of deviance? Which consequences of substance abuse do people other than the abusers themselves most often experience?

> How do notions of deviance or arguments regarding substance abuse play out in the **political arena**? Can you identify typical arguments about substance abuse that have been raised by members of political parties on different parts of the political spectrum?

> Can you identify **spiritual and/or metaphysical** consequences of substance abuse? What kinds of spiritually oriented programs have been developed to address the issue of substance abuse?

Step 2: Progressing from Questions to Potential Claims

In consideration of the questions that arise while applying the topoi of definition, comparison and contrast, origins and consequences, reasons for and against, possibility, and values, Step 2 asks you to develop answers to some of the questions posed during Step 1. As you answer those questions, you can frame those responses as claims that supply the argument of your essay.

QUESTIONS	CLAIMS
DEFINITION	
What parts can substance abuse be divided into? *How does the categorization of different substances affect whether we view them as causing substance abuse?*	While substance abuse can result from misuse of prescription medication, legally available substances, or illicit drugs, the abuse of illegal substances results in the greatest degree of social deviancy because it compounds the propagation and consumption of illicit products.
How has the term "social deviance" changed over time? *What might that change signify for the purposes of this argument?*	The shifting focus of social deviancy from legal to illegal drugs over the past century more accurately reflects the truly wicked issues associated with the deviance of users who choose to use prohibited substances rather than those who abuse otherwise legal substances.
COMPARISON AND CONTRAST	
Are certain substances "worse" in regards to social deviance? Why?	The abuse of prescription medications by those for whom the medicines are not prescribed create a system in which those who legitimately need those medicines face greater scrutiny in acquiring those medications; therefore, they represent a particularly devious example of substance abuse.
What practices comprise our consideration of "social deviance"? *How are those forms of deviancy related to substance abuse? How are they different?*	While the issue of substance abuse as it relates to social deviancy is an important problem to explore, placing the blame so readily on those substances as a cause of deviancy neglects the underlying mental and economic health issues that lead people to abuse drugs.
ORIGINS AND CONSEQUENCES	
What comes before substance abuse?	In order to address substance abuse as a society, we must first turn out attention to the culture of scarcity that leads abusers to self-medicate using illicit substances.
What are the social consequences of substance abuse?	By treating the issue of substance abuse as a criminal matter, we foster a vicious circle in which substance abusers who are labeled as criminals face greater barriers to reintegration into society and escalate the problems that led to the original offense.
What sort of long-term changes or effects will substance abuse lead to?	If substance abuse continues to be ignored as a social health issue, the medical emergencies of overdose victims will place a larger strain on the healthcare system, further preventing adequate care of other patients.

QUESTIONS	CLAIMS
REASONS FOR AND AGAINST	
Why would one argue in favor of the idea that substance abuse represents a legitimate form of social deviancy? *What factors might influence them to make that argument?*	In order to ensure substantial response to the problems of substance abuse, it is necessary to persuade legislators to the major effects that substance abuse has on social welfare.
Why would one argue against this premise?	By labeling abusers of illicit substances as criminals, we shift the focus away from resolving the public health issue of substance abuse and cause people to be fearful of the ramifications of being caught abusing substances.
POSSIBILITY	
Is it possible to resolve the issue of substance abuse in society? *If yes, how?* *If no, why not?*	While abuse of illicit substances seems to be declining thanks in part to the persistent and concerted efforts of antidrug campaigns, abuse of less stigmatized yet more insidious substances (e.g., coffee and alcohol) seems to be on the rise.
What would prevent social deviancy from happening even if one were to engage in substance abuse?	It seems improbable to suggest that we can eradicate substance abuse in any society, but creating greater avenues of support for those suffering from various substance abuse issues can place less strain on the justice and healthcare systems and offer more avenues toward rehabilitation.
VALUES	
*In what ways are definitions of deviance and perspectives on substance abuse determined or informed by our **ethical/moral** standards or accepted social norms?*	The religious and social moralist movements of the nineteenth century continue to have a strong level of influence on social discussions of substance abuse and the association of those suffering from addiction as having committed moral failures. We must first adopt a critical approach to that attitude if we are to explore the issue of substance abuse from a more appropriate perspective.
Many argue that society ultimately bears the burden of substance abuse. *How is **society** implicated in definitions of deviance?* *Which consequences of substance abuse do people other than the abusers themselves most often experience?*	While rehabilitation programs and support groups for substance abuse have undeniable value, some individuals avoid joining them, despite guaranteed anonymity, for fear of identifying themselves as socially deviant. The fear of that label prevents earlier intervention.

As this exercise demonstrates, the process of applying categorical questions helps writers to break down an argument into its parts, to select the questions that are most helpful to constructing an argument, and to move from a broad argument about substance abuse and social deviancy to a narrower framework in which one can make specific claims about a topic. Using the topoi to generate ideas for an argument may also help you determine what claims are more interesting for you to explore as you move toward drafting a Points-to-Make list.

The Pentad

The five terms of Kenneth Burke's Pentad resemble the journalistic "Five Ws" (who, what, when, where, why):

act   names what took place, in thought or deed

agent   names the doer of the act, whether person, force, or concept

agency   names the manner or means of the act

scene   names the background of the act, the situation in which it occurred: spatiotemporal but also social, moral, psychological, etc.

motive   names the purpose of the action

However, the Pentad represents a world view that is radically different from that implicit in the Five Ws. The latter heuristic presupposes a more materialistic or positivistic outlook, one that has come to be associated with the traditional journalistic commitment to describing "just the facts." The Pentad, on the other hand, sees events as *motivated*, as actions rather than motions. Because it privileges the importance of human motivation, the Pentad is particularly well-suited to the analysis of human events or social issues. Furthermore, as Burke suggests in *A Grammar of Motives*, the five simple terms of the Pentad permit a complexity of analysis offered by few other heuristics:

> Our term, agent, for instance, is a general heading that might, in a given case, require further subdivision, as an agent might have his act modified (hence partly motivated) by allies (co-agents) or enemies (counter-agents). Again, under agent, one could place any personal properties that are assigned a motivational value, such as "fear," "malice," "the will," "intuition," or "responsibility." A TSA officer might treat the body as a property of the agent (an expression of disposition, indicating harmlessness or hostility), whereas a full-body X-ray machine would treat it as scenic (a purely objective material). Airline passengers are obviously sentient beings who have deliberately chosen to travel (that is, agents), yet in their accumulation they constitute a social scene, with its own peculiar set of motivational properties.

> War may be treated as an agency, insofar as it is a means to an end; as a collective act, subdivisible into many individual acts; as a motive, in schemes proclaiming a cult of war. For the man inducted into the army, war is a scene, a situation that motivates the nature of training; and in mythologies war is an agent, or perhaps a super-agent, in the figure of the war god.

Sample Brainstorming List Using Pentad

The following brainstorming list could be used to develop ideas in response to a prompt issued in a Writing 150 section connected to a globalization thematic or a thematic pertaining to identity and diversity:

Is the use of racial profiling an appropriate way to protect national security in a time of terrorist threat to the United States?

A single concept can often be ascribed to multiple terms, illustrating the versatility and complexity offered by this heuristic.

ACTS (THAT INVOLVE REFERENCE TO RACIAL PROFILING)		
News conferences regarding terrorist activities	Immigration debates or border dispute	Airport security checks
Discussions or media coverage of war efforts abroad	Legal actions/court findings	Wearing of particular clothing that identifies one as part of a suspect ethnic group
AGENTS (THE PEOPLE, FORCES, OR CONCEPTS THAT PROMPT REFERENCE TO RACIAL PROFILING)		
Police	News commentators	Immigrants
Xenophobia	Civil rights groups (counter)	Politicians
Nativists	Scholars/researchers	Attorneys
Activists (counter)	Refugees	Nationalism
AGENCIES (MEANS BY WHICH DISCUSSION OR REPRESENTATION OF RACIAL PROFILING IS INVOKED)		
Newspapers and magazines	Television shows	Airport security checks
Political discourse	Civil rights litigation	Surveillance systems (e.g., facial recognition)
SCENE (SITUATIONS IN WHICH RACIAL PROFILING IS OFTEN INVOKED)		
Times of terrorist threats to "homeland" security	Anniversary of 9/11	Immigration disputes
Moments of national fear and anxiety	Media reports/coverage	Airport security checks
Traffic violations	Television (e.g., *America's Most Wanted*)	Movies (portrayals of "typical" criminals or terrorists)
MOTIVE (WHY RACIAL PROFILING IS INVOKED)		
To reinforce social norms	To promote awareness of one's environment	To discuss current manifestations of racial/ethnic prejudice
To prevent future terrorist attacks	To codify categories of difference	To blame social problems on The Other

A single concept can often be ascribed to multiple terms, illustrating the versatility and complexity offered by this heuristic.

For example, one might begin with an AGENT or AGENCY, and discuss MOTIVE, e.g.:

What motive might law enforcement officers have to invoke the notion of racial profiling?

This process may lead to another question:

But isn't law enforcement itself a kind of agency? If so, who are the agents? Are officers the only law enforcement agents, or would the media also be included? How about government officials? Does it depend on the circumstances?

This process demands an examination of SCENE, so that a clearer picture of the ACTS can emerge, e.g.:

What motive would law enforcement officers have to invoke the notion of racial profiling in the act of discussing national security? How might the motive change when these agents are talking about immigration? What is the role of scene or circumstance in determining motive?

By juxtaposing different ACTS, AGENCIES, MOTIVES, and AGENTS, you begin to develop a complex view of an issue that might not otherwise develop out of heuristics that overlook the issue of agency. This development of ideas is not linear, but rather recursive—much like the writing process itself.

Points-to-Make Lists

Invention is perhaps the most creative phase of the writing process, and the most crucial: your paper will only be as strong as the fundamental concepts and insights that go into it, and the function of invention is to probe beyond the obvious responses to a question or issue in order to explore ideas that are less certain but more interesting. It follows that invention not only can be, but *should* be, a messy and somewhat unpredictable process. When invention is going well, you will be generating far more material than you could possible use in a single paper, and, in fact, you will *not* want to use *most* of what you come up with during your invention activities. While this process may seem inefficient, wasteful, or even profligate, it's actually both logical and necessary. When ideas spring to mind, they don't come pre-sorted with labels attached—"mediocre," "good," "excellent." Finding an excellent idea or argument is rather like selecting a perfect apple: you have to compare it against many others, choosing the one that seems best and setting aside those that don't seem as good. If you want the best apples, or the best ideas, you will usually have to sort through a large pile to find them.

A points-to-make list helps in that process. During invention, always remain alert for "paragraph points," claims or ideas that have the potential to form the basis for a paragraph you may later want to include in your paper. Whenever such an idea occurs to you, record it on your points-to-make list in a brief phrase or sentence, taking the time to articulate your idea in a manner that will remain comprehensible. (An expression such as "fluorocarbons and comfort" may make sense at the moment, but you should probably record something closer to "our cultural predisposition to comfort contributes directly to the environmental crisis.")

You are unlikely to use all of the claims and ideas you save on your points-to-make list, but the structure of your eventual text will largely reflect the quality of the ideas recorded thereon. The points-to-make list forms the perfect place to begin a rough plan or outline, and, as will be explained in the next section, is also a good place to look for a thesis to use in your paper.

Preparing a Points-to-Make List
Step One

Before you begin your points-to-make list, go back and reread the writing task for the assignment. In any writing situation, you need to compare your prewriting ideas to the actual writing tasks at hand, since it's very easy to drift away from the issue you originally set out to explore.

Step Two

As you generate invention materials, mark the ideas that you think might be most effective in your essay (consider doing this activity with a high-lighter or different colored pen so that you can clearly identify them later, when drafting). At this stage, don't worry if you're interested in a number of different (and possibly unrelated) ideas. In fact, be as inclusive as you can—just develop a primary list of points (ideas and/or opinions you have about the topic) and evidence (facts, examples, and quotes) that you like for your essay.

Step Three

As you review your invention materials, you will begin to think of points you would like to make in your paper; record these on the list in whatever order they come to you. (You can re-arrange their order when you construct your rough plan.) Your list should probably include many different kinds of ideas. On some lines, you will be making very broad points, while on others you'll have examples and small pieces of evidence. In addition, some ideas will be more opinionated while others will be explanatory. Don't worry, and don't try to jump to a thesis statement too soon. Sometimes you need to work with ideas for a while before you finally arrive at what you "really want to say." Be especially aware of the trap that many students fall into—*a mere list of points is not a thesis statement.*

As you record points, you will also begin to note connections and relationships between the points that you wish to make. Try to keep track of these so you can use them in setting up your rough plan.

Step Four

At this point, you may know exactly what you want to argue in your essay. Perhaps from the beginning, you've had a clear opinion on the issue, and now you have numerous supporting points that might get worked into a structure for the paper. On the other hand, perhaps the list has not moved you any closer to what you really want to say. In either case, consider the following questions as a way to focus and narrow your approach to the paper:

1. **Significance:** Why does this question matter? Of course, it matters because it's a class assignment. However, in order to write an effective essay, you need to work out *for yourself* what's at stake in the response that you provide to the writing task. Why should people care about the issue? What do you propose to teach or explain to your audience?

2. **Focus:** What angle/approach seems most comfortable to you? Recognize the potential limitations of a short essay. You can make a very effective point if you find an appropriate angle, but your essay will be hopelessly over-generalized if you don't consider and choose a *limited approach* to the issue. Look at your list of points for that limiting idea.

3. **Opposition:** Whom are you arguing against? Is there an attitude or opinion that you really want to speak against? You needn't—and in most cases, shouldn't—turn your paper into a sustained attack on the opposition, but do think about whether there is an opposition that can help you to clarify and define your central point. In other words, be mindful of counterarguments, even at the prewriting stage.

Developing a Provisional Thesis Idea

During the prewriting process, you should be wary about deciding upon a main point, or thesis, too quickly. An old chess proverb advises that "when you see a good move, *wait!*—there may be a better one," and this adage applies perhaps with even greater force to writing. If during invention you are delving deeply into the ramifications and possibilities of the issue you are considering, then you will inevitably encounter any number of ideas that may seem to have the potential to serve as a thesis for your paper. If you immediately choose the first or second or even third that comes along, you may well be preventing yourself from eventually coming up with an even better idea. Moreover, the first ideas that come to mind are much less likely to offer scope for a fresh and creative argument, since such ideas are usually the first that occur to everyone else as well. Initial ideas are, in fact, very likely to represent just the sort of obvious or clichéd thinking that the invention process is meant to surpass.

At some point, of course, you do need to make at least a provisional commitment to one particular concept or rationale that will serve as the basis for your analysis or argument. In the romantic tradition, this commitment would be made in a sudden flash of inspiration, and sometimes a thesis idea will actually announce itself in that manner. More often, however, a thesis "promotes" itself from among the claims and ideas on your points-to-make list, when you gradually come to the realization that some concept you originally thought might govern a paragraph is actually resonant with many of the most promising points on your list. Napoleon said that each corporal in his army "carried a field marshall's baton in his knapsack," by which he meant that he would promote soldiers from the ranks into the role of officers. When you notice a certain sort of "leadership" potential in one of the items on your points-to-make list, consider whether it might be promoted to higher rank.

In either case, whether your thesis comes in an epiphanic flash or gradually emerges from your points-to-make list, what you want to look for in a good provisional thesis are the qualities of connection and flexibility. Your thesis needs to be able to join—to connect and work with—any of the sub-arguments you want to include in your paper, and it must be flexible enough to permit adjustments and modifications as you actually write the paper. Your thought process doesn't end with the conclusion of your pre-writing, and so you need to select a provisional thesis that will allow your argument or analysis to evolve.

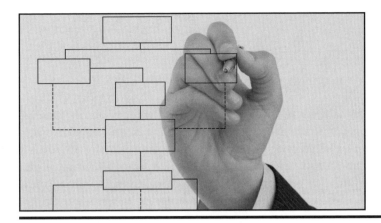

Section **3**

Arrangement

The inscriptive and inventional techniques described in the previous section are crucial to the writing process. By helping you develop and recall information and focus and refine your thinking, such techniques provide a conceptual foundation for your writing. The more time you can spend creating, testing, and "playing" with ideas, the better your paper is likely to be. Again, experienced writers may spend as much as half their time in prewriting activities.

Along with inventing ideas and material, however, prewriting also involves selection and planning. Once you have developed a full and complex set of ideas, arguments, and information, it helps to spend some time organizing it. While it is impossible to foresee every detail of a paper, having a provisional plan will usually let you avoid confusion and save time as you begin writing.

The materials below explain methods to use in moving from inventional activities into a rough draft. They will describe how to construct a points-to-make list from your prewriting materials, how to use this tool to set up a **rough plan** for your paper, and how to create an initial **thesis statement** to guide you in writing your draft.

General Ordering Principles

Arrangement has to do with planning a tentative structure for the paper that reflects the writer's ideas and purpose as these were developed during prewriting. This part of the process is preliminary only, and the goal is to plan the order of your ideas yet remain flexible enough to allow for modification and evolution of these concepts during the process of drafting. Here are some ways to foster good habits of organization:

"Form follows function." Keep in mind that the form or structure of your paper should serve whatever purpose you have in mind, not *vice versa*. The best way to achieve this result is to have a *flexible* plan, one that you can modify as your understanding of what you are writing about evolves and clarifies.

Avoid overly rigid or insufficiently focused approaches to arrangement. The old method of outlining a paper in detail before writing a first draft might work for some people, perhaps, but it is limiting and even paralyzing for others, and it makes writing a process of recording (rather than generating) ideas. The five-paragraph essay is a natural product of a rigid outline and shares the same limitations—even if the five paragraph format is easy to use.

Use conceptual, rather than categorical, organization. When a writer begins drafting a paper before he or she has done enough thinking or prewriting, the result is likely to be organized in a categorical, rather than conceptual, manner. The paper will not so much develop an idea as divide a topic, usually into fairly obvious categories. (Here again, the five-paragraph format encourages just this kind of divisive organization rather than encouraging the development of a logical progression of ideas.) Remember that you should structure your writing to suit a specific purpose, not according to a pre-determined category.

Study the structure of appropriate texts. This practice will not only increase the number of arrangement patterns available to you, but will also help debunk rigid or idealized models of essays, since few published essays meet all the "textbook" requirements for proper structure. While the thesis may not be stated in the last sentence of the first paragraph (and may not be explicitly stated at all), "real" writing can still provide useful lessons on cueing the reader's interpretation, or achieving coherence and cohesion, or any number of similar points.

Writing 150 focuses upon argumentative and analytical writing because these forms of discourse are immediately relevant to the kinds of assignments students will be asked to complete in college and, in most cases, in their professional careers. Both argumentation and analysis privilege critical thinking and, more than many other forms of writing, concern themselves with the careful articulation of concepts and ideas. This commitment to the conceptual entails significant consequences for the ways in which argumentative and analytical essays need to be structured. Ordering principles that are entirely appropriate to other forms of writing may actually be detrimental within the context of argumentation and analysis, so it is helpful to review the main ordering principles in terms of their potential relevance to argumentative or analytical writing.

Chronological order: This principle orders material by time, in the sequence in which events occurred. Chronological order is suitable for narratives—records of persons and actions over time—and a narrative section may sometimes be employed in a piece of argumentative or analytical discourse. However, chronological order is not suitable as the primary organizing principle for most forms of argument and analysis because it becomes very difficult to focus on a concept while having to move back and forth between the chronological elements that sustain a narrative.

Spatial order: Characteristic of descriptive writing, this ordering principle arranges material according to spatial relationships: from left to right, for example, or from near to far, etc. While descriptive writing is often used with argumentation and analysis, spatial ordering is perhaps even less suitable than chronological arrangement for most argumentative or analytical purposes.

Categorical order: While spatial and chronological order directly reflect experiential impressions of space or time, categorical order is somewhat more abstract and marginally more appropriate to concept-centered forms of writing, since categorical organization divides a topic into parts according to some principle of selection. (The five-paragraph essay is the most salient and notorious example of categorical order.) But a selection principle and the categories it defines constitute only very weak kinds of concepts, and although during prewriting a categorical scheme may often serve as a stepping-stone to the recognition of more significant conceptual relationships, categorical organization does not itself provide a sufficient foundation for argumentative or analytical writing.

Conceptual order: Rather than depending upon relationships (whether of time, space, or category) that are fairly predefined and limiting, conceptual organization permits ideas to be linked in a manner that immediately reflects the author's thinking and may be directly governed by his or her purpose or thesis. For these reasons, conceptual ordering provides the most effective means for structuring arguments or analyses.

Arrangement Expectations for Academic Analysis and Argumentation

In the academy, certain protocols are expected in terms of the arrangement of analysis and argumentation, and these will be suggested for your use in Writing 150. First, academic analysis often implies a structure for essays that begins with an introduction in which the thesis typically appears, a body of text that argues on behalf of the thesis, and a conclusion that demonstrates the validity of the thesis and suggests directions for further inquiry.

Examining each of these parts more closely, a thesis presents one position on an issue while at the same time recognizing that other positions exist. That is, a thesis implies the existence of opposing points of view. It accepts the possibility of differing viewpoints because that is the nature of the discourse into which academic writers enter. Few issues that you will encounter in your course work at the university are so one-sided that no opposing position is permitted, and your thesis in any paper ought to acknowledge this complexity.

The thesis is developed through logical analysis and argumentation presented in the body of the paper. This process of development should provide a transparent, straightforward explanation as to why your thesis is plausible on the basis of reason and evidence. Of course, you may also support your thesis by providing appropriate counterarguments in response to opposing positions.

Finally, analysis is succeeded by a conclusion that does more than merely restate your thesis. It also demonstrates the significance of your position (that has been shown to be true), and it offers further questions that should be addressed in any subsequent treatment of the subject as well as additional lines of inquiry that could prove fruitful.

Limitations of the Five-Paragraph Format

While the five-paragraph essay might serve as a tool for attaining some measure of success on certain standardized writing examinations, it is the rhetorical equivalent of training wheels on a bicycle. Like training wheels, the five-paragraph format may help you get started, but it will very soon begin to hinder any further progress and it virtually ensures that you will never win any races.

Because the five-paragraph format is so widely taught in American high schools, and because it can be so limiting within the context of college writing tasks, it is important to be aware of some of the reasons it should be avoided:

1. The five-paragraph format is intentionally artificial; the format depends entirely upon a categorical scheme of organization that simply divides any topic into three sections, which effectively discourages critical thought on the topic at hand; it is seldom seen outside the standardized exam context and almost never used in newspapers, journals, books, or any form of academic discourse.

   › Since the structure of the five-paragraph paper is, by design, predetermined, it discourages any inclination to recognize, learn, or implement essay-specific techniques of arrangement.

   › Because the thesis of a classic five-paragraph essay simply asserts three points that are largely unrelated, the format does not foster thought or insight, but instead undermines the entire exploratory notion of prewriting in general and of invention in particular.

2. The five-paragraph format has neither the flexibility nor the range to address the complexity of most college writing assignments.

   › By relying on a wholly predictable pattern of development and by mandating that the thesis be repeated in the conclusion (after a span of only three paragraphs), the five-paragraph format is not appropriate for an academic/higher education audience as it is likely to not only insult the intelligence of the reader, but also ignore the reader's needs and interests in the nuances of the issue.

   › WRT150 is a course focused on writing and critical reasoning. It requires writers to exercise their rhetorical muscles, so to speak. The five-paragraph essay, however, is largely arhetorical in that it fails to engage its readers—or worse, its writer.

3. Finally, the five-paragraph format stifles the creativity that is necessary for good critical writing and encourages poor writing habits:

   › Because the structure of the five-paragraph essay is set in stone, it precludes any attempt at global revision.

   › By making it not only possible but also advantageous for the writer to employ the first ideas that come to mind, the five-paragraph essay undermines the epistemological function of writing and removes the need for imagination or creativity.

Global Structure

The global structure of your paper—sometimes referred to as its macro-structure—is the framework around which you organize the thesis, introduction, evidence, other supporting paragraphs, and conclusion. It is the schema for presenting your arguments to your reader, and it should involve careful consideration of the manner in which you arrange its elements. Two principal reasons exist for this. First, an ill-considered structure will convey a sense of disorganization to readers, and this will weaken your credibility. Second, the structure that you adopt allows you to marshal your main themes in a manner most conducive to persuading your audience.

A writer may be tempted to begin writing as soon as he or she has an initial sense of what needs to be said. After all, the paper won't write itself, and one must begin at some point. Still, resist this temptation, for an essay dashed off in haphazard fashion may get done, but it likely won't be finished in a way that will please either its author or readers. Time spent at the outset in considering the structure that you wish to adopt is well worth it, as it will provide an anchor around which you can build an effective essay. A well-considered structure also allows the writer a bit of psychological comfort during the writing process, for it eliminates some of the doubt and anxiety that often accompany a work-in-progress. You won't wonder as much about what you want to say and how you will say it, because you will already have come up with a strategy precisely to address these concerns.

The material that follows in this section suggests some guidelines for an overall structure for your paper.

Thesis Development

The Meaning, Function, and Creation of a Thesis

The term thesis comes from the Greek word for "putting" or "positioning." A thesis simply declares your stance on whatever issue you're discussing. Most commonly it will be a single sentence, although it may be longer. And while a thesis statement often appears at the beginning of an essay, it may also be located elsewhere. Sometimes it may even be implicit and not directly stated.

Its task is to form the core of an argument—the unifying principle—that holds an entire essay together. It is the one assertion that puts forward the primary contention of the essay, as opposed to minor themes and points of argument. A strong thesis can help you develop your own perspective on an issue, because instead of just writing about a controversy, you're actually adding something to the discussion about it. Further, a thesis can keep you on track, as it lends a point of reference to which you can constantly refer as you write. In short, it is the assertion as to what your essay will do, the commitment that you've made to yourself and the reader.

Naturally, not all writing requires a thesis, because it constitutes more than simply a purpose. A thesis usually demarks a strong argumentative position. A letter, short story, or any narrative form of writing typically doesn't necessitate that you establish a clear and particular position on an issue. However, most of the academic writing that you will do in college as well as in graduate or professional school—from expository papers to research projects—requires that you adopt a definite position. For this sort of writing a thesis allows you to state that position unequivocally.

You should develop a thesis tentatively and gradually. That is, an effective thesis ought to flow out of your expanding knowledge of a topic as you study and think extensively about it. At the outset of a writing project, you may *think* you know what your position is going to be on the issue at hand. Still, that position may change—indeed, you ought to be open to such change—as you delve more deeply into the issue. In short, your understanding of a controversy should be more profound at the end of your writing process than it was at the beginning, and that, in turn, may cause a change in your initial thesis. So begin with a rough provisional thesis and then hone and sharpen it as you work through various drafts of your paper.

The Characteristics of a Good Thesis Statement

An effective thesis states your position on an issue in clear and definite language. The reader should never be in doubt as to the stance that you are advocating.

It should also be limited in scale, a main point or two that you will develop and reference throughout your essay in a close and specific manner.

In addition, your thesis ought to take a side and attempt to do so in an original way. Avoid canards and bromides—in other words, try to stake out relatively fresh ground in your argument, if that is possible.

In academic discourse, precise expression and nuanced meaning count for a great deal. It follows that thesis claims and other sorts of assertions tend to be carefully qualified in academic analysis and argumentation. In these forms of writing, positions seldom devolve into simplistic certainties supported by absolute assertions (e.g., that something is always the case, or that all of the evidence points to one conclusion). Reality is usually more complicated than that, and your wording should reflect that circumstance.

Ironically, while the thesis is usually the first thing that you write when outlining your argument, you actually must know what your argument will be before you can effectively write it. So begin with a preliminary thesis that you realize may require revision as you delve deeper into your paper. If the focus of your argument changes as your paper progresses, then you must be prepared to change your thesis to reflect this change.

Some Examples of Weak and Strong Theses

The presence of a clearly defined position on a topic:

Poor   The merits of liberal education have been debated for centuries, and even today there are both costs and benefits associated with such a broad-based education.

Better   The merits of liberal education have been debated for centuries, but even in today's highly technological society the benefits of such a broad-based education outweigh the costs.

An assertion of one specific, unified idea:

Poor   In the long run, liberal education will return the money students must invest in it, and it helps produce more moral individuals.

Better   The investment of time and money that liberal education requires rewards a student with a broader range of practical skills than cheaper, specialized schools offer. *broad*

Poor   Liberal education is valuable because it creates people who are mature, better at dealing with other cultures, and who learn quickly.

Better *new* — By allowing students time to explore a variety of subjects and methods, liberal education produces members of society who can cope not only in unfamiliar situations, but can also integrate new information into what they already know.

An emphasis on something that will interest, challenge, persuade, or enlighten your audience:

Poor   Although I know that I might get into med school faster if I went through a pre-med program, I'm glad that I chose to spend my years at USC majoring in political science.

Better   Even students who know exactly which profession they want to enter benefit more from four years of liberal arts education than from a three-year preprofessional program.

Poor   Liberal education is valuable because it builds well-rounded students.

Better   Liberal education may not produce students who are more intelligent than average college graduates, but it does produce students who are trained to use what they do know in a wide variety of situations and are prepared to learn about what they don't know.

A limited scope that is tailored to the specific assignment:

Poor   Since its inception during the Enlightenment, liberal education has never actually fulfilled its promise to create better human beings.

Better   Whether or not liberal education ever did fulfill its promise to create more moral human beings, in today's self-centered society it has clearly failed in this goal.

The presence of clear language and specific terms:

Poor   The education of a student through liberal means will in turn result in people who have a greater ability to return some aspect of their received training to others.

Better   Liberal education produces students who are prepared to use their knowledge and skills to help those who have had fewer economic advantages than themselves.

Traps to Avoid When Constructing a Thesis

Lists, which often lead to vague and disjointed analysis or argumentation.

e.g.,   Television networks are guilty of marketing violent programming to young audiences despite copycat incidents and general desensitization to violence, failing to provide a ratings system that consistently and accurately informs the public about the nature and possible effects of this programming, and seeking to create even more violent programming in order to increase profits.

A simple statement of fact, which may invoke no debate or controversy.

e.g.,   A clean and self-sustaining environment is good for the earth and all of its inhabitants. (Who would disagree with this banality?)

An unexplained stance, or a poorly defined position.

e.g.,   College athletics have gotten out of hand. (How so? In what way? For what reasons?)

A thesis assuming the form of a question, often interpreted as a rhetorical one that doesn't require a response.

e.g.,   Why does filmed entertainment so often display gratuitous sex and violence?

An off-topic thesis.

e.g.,   Reality television degrades American culture by celebrating superficiality, materialism, and a cheapened notion of love. (When, in fact, the prompt asks why reality television has become such a staple of the networks in the last three years.)

Superfluous phrases that produce only arch prose.

e.g.,   In this paper I will advance my opinion, which is that the Greek system on college campuses has become redundant and antiquated, a state of affairs that I will demonstrate.

A Method for Testing Thesis Statements: The Sheridan Baker Approach

Analytical and argumentative writing both depend upon claims. A thesis represents the main claim of an essay, but that thesis will be developed by any number of supporting, or "paragraph-level," claims. It is therefore useful to have a reliable method for developing test claims, assertions which you may (or perhaps may not) want to include in your paper. This is the function of the following procedure. Using it, you can quickly generate potential thesis or paragraph claims. Most of these, of course, will likely be discarded as you test their relevance and possible usefulness to your argument, but this process of testing, discarding, and revising will eventually lead to a set of claims—a provisional thesis and perhaps several paragraph-level cueing statements—that will constitute an initial conceptual structure for your paper. As you go on to draft your paper, this structure may shift, of course, and your thesis and paragraph claims are likely to evolve and become more incisive as you gain a better understanding of what you really want to argue.

While this procedure is only a first step toward the kind of mature thesis that you will want to characterize your take-home writing, its ease and reliability also make it useful when you have to write short essays under time pressure during midterm or final examinations.

The Sheridan Baker Thesis Machine *

Step 1: **TOPIC**

State the topic under consideration.

a. tuition

b. roommates

c. movies

Step 2: **ISSUE**

State the specific issue in the form of a debating proposition.

a. Resolved: Tuition charges should be waived for all college students.

b. Resolved: The university should assign roommates.

c. Resolved: Action movie heroes represent good role models for college students.

Step 3: **POSITION + RATIONALE (because-clause)**　　　　　　　　[ROUGH THESIS]

*Using a **because**-clause, convert the resolution into a sentence that states your position on the issue and provides a **main rationale** for that position.*

a. Tuition charges should be waived for all college students because financial hardship prevents many students from concentrating on their studies.

b. The university should assign roommates because freshmen often don't know any potential roommates on campus when they first arrive.

c. Action movie heroes represent positive role models for college students because they exemplify persistence, focus and determination.

Step 4: **POLISH AND QUALIFY** (**although**-clause) [THESIS]

*Refine the rough thesis: Add any qualifications (**although**-clauses are good for this) and consider dropping overt use of **because**.*

a. Financial hardship, a common consequence of high tuition charges, prevents many students from concentrating on their studies.

b. Although students sometimes prefer living on campus with friends, the university should assign roommates because freshmen often don't know any potential roommates when they arrive.

c. Although many people are injured and murdered in action films, the heroes represent positive role models for college students by embodying important values like persistence, focus and determination.

Step 5: **REVERSE AND TEST**

Test your faith in the thesis and expose potential counterarguments by reversing your position.

a. Financial aid is a viable option to assist students in paying university tuition; student loans and other forms of assistance teach students about financial independence and fiscal responsibility.

b. Although some first-year college students find that roommate assignments reduce anxiety, most students prefer to select a roommate based on common courses or shared interests.

c. Action movie heroes are mindless barbarians who represent no positive or redeeming qualities or characteristics.

* This procedure is based on material originally presented in Sheridan Baker's *Practical Stylist*.

Simple and Complex Conceptual Structures

An analytical or argumentative essay should provide the reader with a clear sense of conceptual "architecture," the structure of ideas that constitute the argument. In the early stages of prewriting and planning, this structure is likely to be fairly simple, and often takes the form of a main point or purpose and a list of potential supporting points. The conceptual architecture is likely to be rather dreary, just a long sequence of arguments conjoined by "and":

Main Point, because

$$V$$

and W

and X

and Y

and Z

If not revised to allow greater complexity, this sort of conceptual structure will most likely produce a paper that is both "listy" and dull, and one that ignores a great many conceptual relationships that could make the paper more insightful, more convincing, and more interesting.

Ross Winterowd in "The Grammar of Coherence" describes a straightforward technique for achieving a conceptual architecture that more adequately addresses the complexity and contrasts to be found in most argumentative issues. Winterowd points out that the coordinating conjunctions that govern the ways sentences may be combined are also relevant to the conceptual relationships that exist between most paragraphs: a sequence of two paragraphs may be "X *and* Y," but it can also be "X *or* Y," "X *for* Y," "X *so* Y," "X *yet* Y," or "X *but* Y." Keeping these additional sequencing options in mind will not only help you achieve a more interesting conceptual architecture in your paper, but will also prompt you to explore alternatives (or), to look for causal relationships (for, so), and to remain alert to the need for counterargument or concessions (yet, but).

Rough Plans and Outlines

What Is a Rough Plan?

A rough plan is simply a quick outline or sketch that identifies the main sections of a proposed piece of writing. It is not a detailed or fully developed outline. Since the paragraph is the main conceptual and structural unit of an essay, a rough plan usually takes the form of a paragraph outline.

What Is a Rough Plan Good For?

A rough plan will not write the paper for you: it will not provide a shortcut around the thought and labor that solid writing requires, nor will it act as some sort of blueprint that, once completed, will let you "assemble" an essay from the prefabricated sections it describes. Good writing is too creative and dynamic for that. Even with a plan that is well considered and carefully structured, you will find that your thinking continues to evolve as you draft and revise the actual paper, and you should therefore be prepared to reconsider and modify your original plan as your writing proceeds.

What a rough plan *can* do, particularly when you are facing the deadlines associated with most writing projects in college and professional life, is to help you focus your paper and avoid some unnecessary difficulties. By marking out a relevant direction for your paper, a rough plan permits you to engage the complexities of your issue in an organized manner; moreover, by helping you to identify directions that are irrelevant or unnecessary to your main purpose, a rough plan can spare you the time and energy that would otherwise be wasted pursuing these directions in a full-scale draft.

How Do I Construct a Rough Plan?

1. Once you determine a main purpose for your paper, review your prewriting materials and select those items relevant to your main idea. (A good points-to-make list is especially helpful in this regard.)

2. Arrange these items in a logical (but provisional) sequence of points.

3. State each point so it indicates the purpose of the proposed paragraph: tell what the paragraph will do to advance the paper's main idea or overall purpose, not merely what the paragraph will be "about."

4. The plan may also provide some sense of how different paragraphs will be developed—the kinds of support or analysis you will use to develop the paper's main idea or argument.

5. Finally, check the plan to see how well it holds together and whether you wish to make any changes to it. The following examples indicate some of the problems to look for in evaluating your rough plan.

A Workable Rough Plan

The sequence of paragraphs described below represents a workable rough plan. In using this plan to guide the initial draft of a paper, you will almost certainly encounter problems, and therefore will have to make modifications and additions to the plan. However, in reviewing the plan it is nonetheless possible to gain some confidence in the overall focus of the proposed paper and in the likelihood of developing a coherent argument in support of the thesis. Having such an overview makes the task of completing a draft somewhat less daunting and reduces the risk that a great deal of time will be spent producing a paper that eventually falls apart.

The following rough plan was developed in response to a prompt used in a course with the thematic "Globalization: Current Issues and Cross-Cultural Perspectives":

How might global critical reasoning help reapproach a particular issue or set of issues in globalization today?

¶1 WHAT INTRODUCTION WILL DO:		¶5 WHAT PARAGRAPH WILL DO:	
Establish that human decision-making process is rarely dominated by empathy. Other yearnings overwhelm intrinsic generosity. Explains why "universality" is so rare. Engage with Edward Said quote. Make connection that empathy does not emerge often enough to significantly reduce society's ills… Provisional Thesis: approaches to ameliorating the dire situations that rely on empathy are generally unrealistic, but we can harness the positive by-product of individual achievement to act as an interim solution to address problems in developing countries.		Pivot away from empathy. Show humans are by no means primarily altruistic, but they are incredibly driven, passionate, and productive when it comes to achieving their own goals. Engage with Rabindranath Tagore quote here, "scientists, philosophers, saints achieved" "for all mankind." Explain that individual achievement can have positive side effects that benefit a larger community rather than just the immediate individual. Reinforce point that we all have our strengths, and by utilizing them to their fullest extents, we passively contribute to society.	
¶2 WHAT PARAGRAPH WILL DO:		¶6 WHAT PARAGRAPH WILL DO:	
Show that our idealistic approach to problem solving is often the limiting perspective that prevents us from solving the selfsame problems. Give background analysis on how efforts that focus on fostering a more altruistic and generous attitude take a long time to effect. Solutions to global issues that first necessitate some sort of partial enlightenment of humanity are unattainable. This may seem unreasonable.		Concede a major caveat to this theory: oftentimes, the side effects of individual achievement are more harmful than helpful. Businesses may neglect a customer; politicians may lend an ear to lobbyists, etc…Recognize that little can be done directly to negate their presence. The solution, however, is to maximize the side effects of achievement that are positive and to provide more opportunities for people to produce side effects of the beneficial type. Essentially, positive side effects can be engineered and redirected in order to most benefit regions in need.	

¶3	WHAT PARAGRAPH WILL DO:	¶7	WHAT PARAGRAPH WILL DO:
	Give context explaining why lack of empathy is normal. Creating empathy involves stepping outside of our comfort zones. Engage with Said quote here on "easy certainties" and "taking a risk." Although often not obvious, factors, such as the comfort provided us by our homes and communities, the lack of language barrier within our local contexts, and the stability of society within developed countries make empathy with others difficult.		Make argument here: a form of global reasoning can allow us to harness society's individual members' drive to achieve for themselves to subliminally benefit others on a global scale. In short, allow humanity to be selfish, but harness that the energy they generate in working for themselves and apply it to benefit the world. Give current examples—restaurants donate proceeds to charity, also, microfinance—investors feel involved and other small businesses benefit. Suggest idea about tech companies hosting tech competitions where the challenge revolves around building products for citizens in need. Furthermore, existing incentives systems can be streamlined by the application of technology.
¶4	WHAT PARAGRAPH WILL DO:	¶8	WHAT CONCLUSION WILL DO:
	Make connection that our identities are intimately tied to the aforementioned certainties. So there are threats to questioning one's own identity and being willing redefine it. Give examples—religious beliefs or nationalism. If we go down that road, we begin to second-guess the person we have always assumed we were. For these reasons, it is unrealistic to expect humanity to change its nature within a short span of time.		Emphasize that there simply isn't enough empathy at the moment to actively solve the problems that humanity currently faces. Issues like global poverty, disease, and conflict will not wait for humanity to augment its compassion. The interim solution is not to engineer society, but rather the system that surrounds it to make maximum use of its ambition.

Another Way to Visualize a Rough Plan: The Block Diagram

The paragraphs making up an essay may be diagrammed in such a way as to show the relationship between the main line of argument (the thesis or main purpose of the paper) and the paragraph-level points or claims used to advance it. A schematic overview of this sort may help in spotting problems in the paragraph sequence. These may include places where the paragraph sequence may need to be reordered or places where there seems to be a gap or "leap of logic" between the paragraph-point and the main line of argument.

Thesis Claim

Approaches to ameliorating the dire situations that rely on empathy are generally unrealistic, but we can harness the positive by-product of individual achievement to act as an interim solution to address problems in developing countries.

Supporting Argument "U"

Show that our idealistic approach to problem solving is often the limiting perspective that prevents us from solving the selfsame problems. Give background analysis on how efforts that focus on fostering a more altruistic and generous attitude take a long time to effect. Solutions to global issues that first necessitate some sort of partial enlightenment of humanity are unattainable. This may seem unreasonable.

Supporting Argument "V"

Give context explaining why lack of empathy is normal. Creating empathy involves stepping outside of our comfort zones. Engage with Said quote here on "easy certainties" and "taking a risk." Although often not obvious, factors, such as the comfort provided us by our homes and communities, the lack of language barrier within our local contexts, and the stability of society within developed countries make empathy with others difficult.

Supporting Argument "W"

Make connection that our identities are intimately tied to the aforementioned certainties. So there are threats to questioning one's own identity and being willing to redefine it. Give examples—religious beliefs or nationalism. If we go down that road, we begin to second-guess the person we have always assumed we were. For these reasons, it is unrealistic to expect humanity to change its nature within a short span of time.

49

Supporting Argument "X"

Pivot away from empathy. Show humans are by no means primarily altruistic, but they are incredibly driven, passionate, and productive when it comes to achieving their own goals. Engage with Rabindranath Tagore quote here, "scientists, philosophers, saints achieved" "for all mankind." Explain that individual achievement can have positive side effects that benefit a larger community rather than just the immediate individual. Reinforce point that we all have our strengths, and by utilizing them to their fullest extents, we passively contribute to society.

Supporting Argument "Y"

Concede a major caveat to this theory: oftentimes, the side effects of individual achievement are more harmful than helpful. Businesses may neglect a customer; politicians may lend an ear to lobbyists, etc...Recognize that little can be done directly to negate their presence. The solution, however, is to maximize the side effects of achievement that are positive and to provide more opportunities for people to produce side effects of the beneficial type. Essentially, positive side effects can be engineered and redirected in order to most benefit regions in need.

Supporting Argument "Z"

Make argument here: a form of global reasoning can allow us to harness society's individual members' drive to achieve for themselves to subliminally benefit others on a global scale. In short, allow humanity to be selfish, but harness that the energy they generate in working for themselves and apply it to benefit the world. Give current examples—restaurants donate proceeds to charity, also, microfinance—investors feel involved and other small businesses benefit. Suggest idea about tech companies hosting tech competitions where the challenge revolves around building products for citizens in need. Furthermore, existing incentives systems can be streamlined by the application of technology.

A Questionable Rough Plan

The five-paragraph format often promulgated in American high schools is extremely simple and thus easy to teach and to learn. It does not, however, provide the flexibility or range necessary for effective college or professional writing, something that may be seen in its complete absence from academic or professional journals. Because the five-paragraph format encourages the writer simply to categorize a topic into three parts, it can actually hinder the critical and conceptual thinking that makes for strong college writing.

ROUGH PLAN		POTENTIAL PROBLEMS
¶1	WHAT INTRODUCTION WILL DO:	
	Cues Main Idea: That a transnational perspective would provide a way to re-approach the human rights issues of child soldiers, gender equality, and access to health care.	Main idea (transnational perspective) is simply tethered to three categories of human rights abuses.
¶2	WHAT PARAGRAPH WILL DO:	
	Explain how transnationalism can help address problem of children being conscripted into military service.	Paragraph proposes a "transnational" argument on a first category of evidence, but with a very "flat" conceptual architecture: just the main claim and this evidence, but without any paragraph-level concept that would develop (rather than simply apply) the main idea of a transnational perspective.
¶3	WHAT PARAGRAPH WILL DO:	
	Explain how transnationalism can help address problem of gender inequality.	Paragraph applies transnational perspective to a second category of evidence. Note that the main claim or thesis is simply being repeated, not developed.
¶4	WHAT PARAGRAPH WILL DO:	
	Explain how a transnationalist perspective can help provide better access to health care.	Once more, paragraph simply applies the main idea to yet another body of evidence. The thesis is being repeated rather than developed.
¶5	WHAT CONCLUSION WILL DO:	
	Restate the idea that a transnational perspective has potential effectiveness in addressing the issues of child soldiers, gender inequality, and inaccessible health care.	Conclusion merely restates the paper's categorical thesis, adding little to the paper's significance or to the reader's understanding.

Spotting Problems in Rough Plans

In analyzing a rough plan, it is possible to identify a number of potential structural problems and thus avoid the large expenditure of time that otherwise would be wasted on writing, and then having to repair, a seriously flawed rough draft. Six common problems are illustrated below:

1. Paragraph without a point;

2. Paragraph point irrelevant to thesis;

3. Paragraph presenting unnecessary summary;

4. Paragraph presenting multiple points;

5. Paragraph sequence out-of-order;

6. Redundant paragraphs.

Each of the following examples addresses the same prompt used in the section above on "A Workable Rough Plan"; the main line of argument or analysis in all cases is this:

We can re-approach significant issues affecting global security by establishing an autonomous space or presence on the web within which a spectrum of knowledgeable moderate voices, self-regulated by principles of ethical discourse, might offer a more nuanced and balanced transnational critique of security matters.

Problem	*Potential Problem #1: Paragraph without a Point*	Revision
¶3 WHAT PARAGRAPH WILL *DO*: Show that the Cold War division between the "free world" and the "Soviet bloc" dichotomized international cooperation.	While this claim is true, it is more a statement of fact than an actual point that might be argued and developed in a paragraph. Such facts may be used to provide support for a paragraph, but they don't themselves offer enough room for development. In such cases, the proposed paragraph may be dropped or the material in it may be associated with an appropriate paragraph point (related to some main claim), as is done in the revision shown here.	¶3 WHAT PARAGRAPH WILL *DO*: Analyze ways in which an independent trans-national web authority could help us re-approach security issues [main concept] by disrupting top-down dichotomies [paragraph concept] such as those that arose during the Cold War.

Problem	Potential Problem #2: Point Irrelevant to Thesis	Revision
¶3 WHAT PARAGRAPH WILL *DO*: Argue that establishing a critical transnational web presence will neither compete with nor threaten legitimate social or commercial web modalities.	While this claim is hypothetically plausible, it is not highly relevant to the question of re-approaching global issues. There is, however, potential relevance in the fact that many web modalities, whether legitimate or illegitimate, tend to ignore or distort global issues, something which the proposed revision uses as a jumping-off point.	**¶3** WHAT PARAGRAPH WILL *DO*: Argues that a critical transnational web authority would provide both an alternative and a challenge to web modalities, whether governmental or commercial, that provide simplistic coverage of global security issues.

Problem	Potential Problem #3: Unnecessary Summary	Revision
WHAT PARAGRAPH WILL *DO:* Describe the often shallow and uncritical news coverage of six different examples of global security issues. **WHAT PARAGRAPH WILL** *DO:* Argue, using support from Examples 1, 2, 4, & 6, that a critical transnational web presence could offer more localized and balanced coverage of global security issues. **WHAT PARAGRAPH WILL** *DO:* Argue, using support from Examples 1, 3, 4 that a critical transnational web presence could offer a more nuanced and less biased analysis of global security issues.	In this sequence of three proposed paragraphs, Paragraph 2 gives a complete description of six different examples of global security issues. Paragraphs 3 and 4 then offer distinct, but related, concepts suggesting how a critical transnational web presence might afford better coverage and analysis of the issues described in Paragraph 2. The question to consider is whether it is necessary or useful to describe all the examples before moving into the two subsequent paragraph concepts. Since any argument will have to refer to the examples, the "describe-every-thing-first" approach, the answer is probably "No." Because the reader cannot be reliably expected to retain any detailed recollection of the examples by the time he or she reads the later arguments, any pertinent details will have to be repeated, a redundancy that can easily be avoided simply by moving directly to the point and *there* relating (in that paragraph) whatever details from various examples will be needed to support the claim being made. Avoid summarizing material for later discussion, and don't expect your reader to remember such details and to apply them as you would wish: *show* the reader the details as you argue the point.	**WHAT PARAGRAPH WILL** *DO:* Argue, using support from Examples 1, 2, 4, & 6, that a critical transnational web presence could offer more localized and balanced coverage of global security issues. **WHAT PARAGRAPH WILL** *DO:* Argue, using support from Examples 1, 3, 4 that a critical transnational web presence could offer a more nuanced and less biased analysis of global security issues.

Problem	Potential Problem #4: Paragraph with Multiple Points	Revision
¶4 WHAT PARAGRAPH WILL *DO*: Argue that a transnational critical web presence offers analytical insights into global security issues that cannot be attained because of the inflexibility of national or corporate perspectives and because "local politics" tend to promote a defensive attitude.	This proposed paragraph offers two points, each of which is relevant to the paper's thesis and each of which can be developed with a good deal of supporting material. The question is whether these points might be more effectively discussed independently of one another. "Splitting" such paragraphs usually improves the clarity of your argument and allows you to develop each point more fully.	¶4 WHAT PARAGRAPH WILL *DO*: Argue that a transnational critical web presence can provide a subtlety and depth of analysis unattainable from the much less flexible positions usually taken by nations or multinational corporations. ¶5 WHAT PARAGRAPH WILL *DO*: Argue moreover that a transnational critical web affords a viable means of evading the defensiveness inherent to positions highly influenced by considerations of "local politics."

Problem	Potential Problem #5: Paragraph Sequence Out-of-Order	Revision
¶3 WHAT PARAGRAPH WILL *DO:* Argue that establishing an autonomous transnational web presence will facilitate a productive critique of inherently biased national news sources. **¶4** WHAT PARAGRAPH WILL *DO:* Point out that the spectrum of viewpoints represented in the transnational web presence and the commitment to transparent and ethical discourse practices would together permit more balanced and moderate criticism. **¶5** WHAT PARAGRAPH WILL *DO:* Argue that a critical transnational web presence would provide a model by which national news sources might evolve toward more thoughtful reporting and analysis of security issues.	Here the points made in Paragraphs 3 and 5 are similar: both discuss ways in which a transnational web presence might influence national news sources. Paragraph 4 thus may be seen as separating or interrupting these two related points, which might be stronger if presented to the reader as a sequence. Sometimes this can be accomplished by combining the two paragraphs into one, but in this case, the related points are distinct enough that they may be developed in separate paragraphs. Thus the appropriate revision is to move the disruptive paragraph so that the related paragraphs will function in sequence.	**¶3** WHAT PARAGRAPH WILL *DO:* Point out that the transnational spectrum of viewpoints and its commitment to transparent and ethical discourse practices would lead to a more balanced and moderate critical stance. **¶4** WHAT PARAGRAPH WILL *DO:* Argue that this more tolerant critical stance provides an excellent basis from which to critique the inherent bias of national news sources in covering security issues. **¶5** WHAT PARAGRAPH WILL *DO:* Point out that in addition, a critical transnational web presence provides a model whereby national news sources might evolve toward more nuanced reporting and analysis of security issues.

Problem	Potential Problem #6: Redundant Paragraphs	Revision
¶5 WHAT PARAGRAPH WILL *DO*: Suggest that a critical transnational web presence would advance Edward Said's notion of employing "a single standard for human behavior" in dealing with the challenging security issues related to global warming. **¶6** WHAT PARAGRAPH WILL *DO*: Argue that an independent transnational web authority would also be better positioned to tackle security issues related to disease transmission and invasive species.	These two paragraphs are *doing* nearly the same thing; the only difference between them is in the type of supporting examples each proposes to use. (Compare these paragraphs with Paragraphs 4 and 5 in the previous example, which are making similar but essentially separate arguments.) When paragraphs are redundant—when they perform essentially the same function—it is usually best to combine them into a single paragraph. In this instance both global warming and matters of disease transmission and invasive species may be tucked under the more general concept of environmental security issues.	**¶5** WHAT PARAGRAPH WILL *DO*: Suggest that a critical transnational web presence would advance Edward Said's notion of employing "a single standard for human behavior," one that would apply to rich nations as well as poor ones, in dealing with the challenges posed by various environmental security issues.

The Paragraph

Paragraphs serve a number of functions—logical, psychological, and rhetorical—and the conventions governing their use are not precisely defined. Nevertheless, in one form or another they have proven to be an indispensable structuring device, particularly in expository and argumentative writing, and are therefore an important subject in composition classes. The following activities and explanatory techniques are intended to provide writers with options to use in revising their paragraphs.

Characteristics of a Good Paragraph
A bit of history might give you a new appreciation for the paragraph: before technological advances in the printing process occurring in the seventeenth century, paragraph indentations didn't exist. As a result books were dense, bearing page after page of unbroken text.

Paragraph structure as we know it today was conceived in the nineteenth century, when a Scottish academic, Alexander Bain, developed an "organic paragraph model," in which every part of the paragraph relates to the whole. Bain used the terms **topic sentence**, **unity**, **coherence**, and **development** to describe the characteristics of effective paragraphs.

Bain was a psychologist, and Bain's paragraph model captures a certain psychological reality. Readers generally anticipate that most paragraphs will focus on one primary point (**unity**), that this point will be clearly articulated (often in a **topic sentence**), that the paragraph will hang together in an organized manner, with logical transitions between words and sentences (**coherence**), and that the paragraph point will be elaborated upon and supported (**development**).

Despite these shared expectations, there is no agreed-upon paragraph formula; different arguments require different paragraphing strategies. Still, there *are* some general guidelines for crafting clear, well-organized paragraphs that keep readers engaged:

Unity: A unified paragraph has one primary purpose, or paragraph point, that helps to advance your essay's main point or thesis. Your reader shouldn't have to struggle to decipher paragraph points—early in each paragraph, you should provide the reader with a "cue" as to the paragraph's purpose, and you should concentrate on that purpose as you develop the remainder of the paragraph. If you find yourself drifting away from your paragraph point, then it's time either to begin a new paragraph or to refocus your attention on the purpose of the one at hand.

Cueing: If the reader is to follow the point you wish to make in a paragraph, he or she needs to know what that point is, and that is why it is generally best to cue your paragraph purpose somewhere near the head of the paragraph, often in the first sentence or two. Should you wait longer than that to cue the paragraph purpose, the reader is likely to lose the thread of your argument. On occasion, of course, you may wish to try an inductive approach, in which you lead the reader through evidence that builds to a paragraph point that is not actually stated until late in the paragraph. Such cases are tricky, however, because you still have to provide some sort of topical coherence until the paragraph point is finally enunciated.

Keep in mind that cueing or topic sentences usually need to do three things:

1. indicate the paragraph purpose;

2. indicate how that purpose relates to your thesis; and

last thing 3. provide transitional linkage with the preceding paragraph.

That's a lot for any one sentence to accomplish, and, in practical terms, effective paragraph cueing is generally a matter of sharpening cueing sentences gradually over the course of several drafts.

In the first draft, you may simply introduce the basic claim of the paragraph. In the next draft, you add some language from your thesis concept so that the reader can understand how the paragraph advances your overall arguments. Finally, in a later draft, you consider how the purpose of one paragraph relates to the purpose of the preceding paragraph and add language indicative of this relationship to your topic sentence to provide a sense of transition.

Development: The overall effectiveness of your paragraphs in advancing the thesis of your paper is principally dependent upon the quality of their development: you need to support each paragraph claim with evidence and reasoning sufficient enough to convince your readers of its plausibility. Here, as elsewhere in writing, a nice sense of balance and judgment is important. Since you are already convinced of what you are arguing, you will probably find that you need to provide your reader with more evidence than seems to you necessary to accept the claim; this may be why ineffective paragraphs most often tend to be underdeveloped rather than overdeveloped. But sheer length or bulk does not make a paragraph more convincing, however much such paragraphs may help to pad out the page-length of the paper. Keep in mind a metaphor from carpentry: once a nail has been driven home, you don't keep hammering at it. The same thing is true of paragraphs: once your point has been made, go on to the next.

Some Frameworks for Thinking about Paragraphs
Simple models or metaphors can be helpful when discussing the structure of a paragraph or the sequence of paragraphs. Here are models that may help writers "see" and thus more quickly grasp basic elements of paragraph structure.

The "Cell Model"

The cell provides a very simple metaphor for discussing the paragraph since, like a cell, an expository paragraph contains both a controlling concept or purpose (the "nucleus") and a relatively greater quantity of supporting material. A paragraph with two or more "nuclei" usually needs to be split up, with support being developed for each of the resulting paragraphs. Similarly, a paragraph that is all supporting material needs to be provided with an appropriate cue as to its purpose, or conjoined with a paragraph that already enunciates that purpose.

Sample "Two-Nuclei" Topic Sentence

"A transnational critical web presence offers analytical insights into global security issues that cannot be attained because of the inflexibility of national or corporate perspectives and because 'local politics' tend to promote a defensive attitude."

—from *Rough Plan Potential Problem #4,* page 55

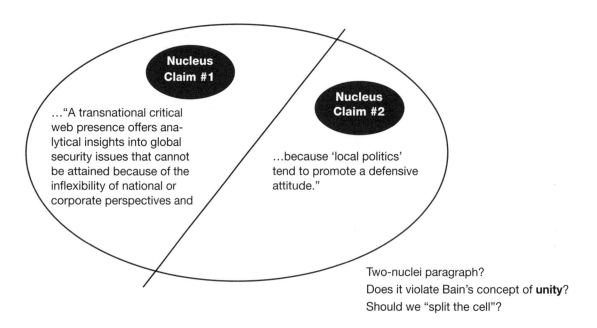

Two-nuclei paragraph?
Does it violate Bain's concept of **unity**?
Should we "split the cell"?

Christensen Paragraph Diagram

Francis Christensen has suggested that the sentences of a paragraph may be diagrammed according to their level of generality. Under this system, the most general sentence of the paragraph is labeled as "1," supporting arguments or examples are labeled as "2" and indented accordingly, and sentences elaborating on the supporting arguments are labeled as "3" and indented even farther. This system of coordinate and subordinate relationships works fairly well with expository writing, perhaps less well with narrative paragraphs. It can help writers spot paragraphs that are underdeveloped (a "1" with only one or two "2s" and no "3s") or uncued (a bunch of "2s" and "3s" with no "1"). Writers should realize that many sorts of well-written paragraphs might not reflect this strict kind of structure. "Pivot" paragraphs, for example, that link one section of related paragraphs with another, will not contain any supporting "2s" or "3s." (The following example is adapted from an article by Karen Springen, "Old Allies in a Timber War," *Newsweek* 24 Sept. 1990: 31.)

1.   In their fight to save the planet, environmentalists have squared off against an erstwhile ally.

   2.   The U.S. Forest Service was chartered nearly a hundred years ago to protect and conserve America's national forests.

   2.   But critics say the agency now takes in billions of dollars by allowing the timber industry to "harvest" 400,000 acres of forest land every year.

      3.   To make matters worse, activists says, the government's replanting program is creating an environmental time bomb.

3. "It took major millennia to get forests established," says Andy Kerr of the Oregon Natural Resources Council, "and then [they] go in and nuke it."

Christensen in Practice: "1, 2, 3" and Your Metaphor-of-Choice

The most important things to remember about Bain, Christensen, and the Cell Model are the concepts they illustrate about good paragraphing. In fact, the paragraphing metaphor a writer uses can be fluid as long as these underlying concepts remain the same. For example, one can think of a sound paragraph as equivalent to a good **football team**:

Claim = Offense; the attack (*argument*) led by the quarterback (*topic sentence*).

Support/Reasoning = Defense; needs to make the offense's score hold up and defend against the offense of the "skeptic" and hope for a turnover (*the ability to change the opinion of the skeptical reader*).

Cueing/Coherence = Special teams; the transitional moments between offense and defense need to be effective (*as do transitional moments between claim and support, between support and analysis, between words and sentences*).

Or a good **song**:

Claim = Melody; the main guitar riff should be catchy and cogent, not boring. Every track on the album needs a new melody (*every paragraph in the paper needs a different claim than the last*).

Support/Reasoning = Rhythm; bass and drums flesh out the melody (*claim*) and give it weight and depth. This allows the song to be played boldly and performed at the Galen Center as part of a national tour, not just open-mic night at Ground Zero (*allows the paper to get "airplay" in the Academic Discourse Community, whereas baseless and unsubstantiated claims will be dismissed*).

Cueing/Coherence = Lyrics; these engage the listener (*reader*) and navigate them through the song by transitioning fluidly from verse to bridge to chorus. Telling a cohesive story makes the song more than just a series of notes (*makes a paper more than just a presentation of facts or data*).

Use the following sample paragraphs to help conceptualize these models, and perhaps try one of your own. Let's use one more seemingly trivial metaphor—the paragraph as a good **sandwich**:

Too Much Filler?

Many low-income Americans are unable to maintain housing costs such as high mortgage payments, which has a direct correlation to the rise in residential foreclosures. According to journalist, Molly Edmonds, the number of foreclosures has reached a record high in the United States (Edmonds). The Mortgage Bankers Association reported that more than 900,000 households are in foreclosure (Edmonds). As Professor of Urban Development, Solomon Poretsky, states, "When low-income people spend the majority of their income on rent, they are only steps away from homelessness" (Poretsky). Low-income individuals are often blamed for being unable to pay their mortgages, but their poor management stems from industry dishonesty and a lack of information. Low introductory mortgage rates often reset at incredibly high values a few years later (Edmiston). Further complicating this problem, "people with low credit scores are the main recipients of subprime mortgages" (Edmonds). If low-income Americans cannot maintain the housing costs tied to their new home, they will end up facing foreclosure and a precarious economic future that could lead to another nationwide recession.

Verdict:

1. Topic sentence
2. evidence/analysis
3. Conceptual arrangement
4. Complex thesis

> "Information Dump" held together with *thin conceptual bread. Messy and overstuffed.*

> An example of too many "3s," per Christensen. Moves from general ("1") to ultra-specific ("3") without any connective tissue ("2").

> Too little sentence-to-sentence coherence, per Bain. The reasoning is lost in a maze of facts, and the reader has trouble following along. Remember, good writing not only cues smoothly between paragraphs, but between sentences, as well.

> Argumentative writing is not a contest to see who can find the most research, just as *a good meal is judged by much more than its raw size.*

Sounds Nice on the Menu, But...?

Though healthcare reform measures like Obamacare attempt to mitigate the effects of poverty by providing affordable plans to low-income individuals, they do little to address the root problem of residential segregation, which can generate unique health problems. Even more so than healthcare access, the physical dichotomy between the white majority and minorities via de facto segregation creates major health disparities. The pernicious existence of residential segregation as a considerably powerful interracial barrier yields an abundance of long-term health risks in segregated neighborhoods. When minorities are isolated in high concentrations in residential areas, they are subject not only to blatant environmental health hazards, but also to the more subtle dangers associated with a lack of health consciousness and with an abundance of high-calorie, low-nutrition food. To combat the disparities created by residential segregation, reform efforts should be directed toward preventative measures that address the environmental and food consumption problems causing illness in low-income neighborhoods.

Verdict:

> Sophisticated and well-phrased claims, but the paragraph lacks any specific anchoring evidence. *Sounds nice on the menu but doesn't pack much flavor…it might be made with gourmet lettuce, but at the end of the day, still just a lettuce sandwich…*

> Many "1s" and "2s" but no "3s," per Christenson. The sentences remain at arm's length, never offering a needed dose of specificity.

> Not enough development, per Bain. Even the most elegant writing will alienate a reader if it doesn't offer concrete support. Note that this is always a potential problem when using hypothetical scenarios for support.

Wish They Served This at EVK?

Rap music contributes to the stereotypes and prejudices that oppress black culture, despite its more socially radical beginnings. When gangsta rap first became a hot commodity in the 1980s, it rightly attempted to challenge the status quo. As Dr. Anthony Pinn, Professor of Humanities and Religious Studies at Rice University, notes, gangsta rap was derived from a desire to undermine the inequality of Reagan/Bush neoliberal capitalism (Pinn 222). The obtaining of "goods" through violence became one of the key components of the genre, as white consumption and increased corporatism became major points of critique in the music. But the more stereotypical the content of the music became, the more white consumers purchased it. Songs depicting the lives and adventures of "authentic" black rappers in "ghetto" culture generated the greatest demand. The rappers who made the most money were those who contributed to the idea of the "black pimp, criminal, ho, trick, drug dealer, bitch, hustler, gangsta, and parolee," cashing in on the trend of glorifying the ghetto lifestyle (Pinn 225). Big music corporations added fuel to the fire by promoting and publicizing those rappers who indulged in the worst stereotypes. This corporate endorsement of stereotypes served a dual purpose: it enriched the corporations themselves, and it excused contemporary social inequalities. As Dr. Christine Reyna, a psychology professor at DePaul University, elucidates, big corporations "often endorse stereotypes in order to justify the existing social system" (Reyna 363). Corporate influence and media coverage thus used rap music to present black people as rulers of their own appalling circumstances, and therefore at fault for their perpetuated social oppression. Promoting images of the "thug rapper" that was born of the struggles of the ghetto allowed the largely white public to satisfy their curiosity about black culture without experiencing any of the suffering linked to the music. The thug rapper's existence and behavior consequently functioned to sustain negative white perceptions of black people as criminals and social outcasts, thereby propagating the prejudice and discrimination that created the ghetto to begin with.

Verdict:

> A balanced mix of claims and evidence, reads smoothly. *Tastes good and relatively easy to digest. Ingredients are nicely layered.*

> Even skeptical readers prefer this, because they can actually understand the argument they are up against. A writer can then anticipate skeptics' counterarguments, and plan rebuttals accordingly.

> "1s," "2s," and "3s" in an appropriate ratio, per Christenson. Writer takes care not to leave any dangling "3s"—facts that have neither been contextualized nor interpreted. Nor are there dangling "1s" or "2s"—claims needing to be matched with specific support.

> Topic sentence, unity, coherence, and development are all present, per Bain.

Specialized Paragraphs: Introductions

Introductions take many forms, but in analytical or argumentative writing, any introduction has two crucial functions: it articulates the issue to be discussed, and it puts the author's thesis or main line of argument into play. Introductions may also provide background or contextual information that may be important for the reader to know if he or she is to be able to follow the arguments made later in the paper. One thing introductions don't do is to begin arguing specific points—that's the function of the body paragraphs that follow.

Here are some ways to introduce or "open" your paper:

Initial ("Blunt Statement") Draft Introductions

To control a piece of writing, you need to have a sense of the main idea or main direction you wish to pursue, and the function of a first-draft introduction is to provide a point of reference that, by enunciating some statement of your main purpose, allows you to shape your essay in a way that develops and supports that purpose. However, in the very act of generating a first draft, you will probably find that your understanding of your topic undergoes (as indeed it should) substantial change. Since this sort of conceptual evolution will usually require you to modify your thesis (and thus your introduction), it makes little sense to waste time crafting a full-fledged introduction before you have finished an entire rough draft of the paper—a complete sequence of body paragraphs.

Thus your initial draft introduction need be nothing more than a blunt statement of your main purpose: "In this paper, I intend to do X." An entire essay can "hang" quite securely from this sort of introduction until you have a chance to revise and expand it. Indeed, the stark clarity of a simple statement of main purpose will help you keep your first draft in much better focus than would the hesitant and vague uncertainty of most introductions produced prior to the paper itself. At best, such introductions represent a kind of "ship-in-the-bottle" writing in which you attempt to work out all your ideas in the cramped space of a single paragraph. If instead you develop your ideas where they should be worked out—in the rough draft of the body of your paper—you may well find that your introduc-tions (when you finally get around to completing them) are not only easier to produce but much more effective. And you will almost certainly find that you have saved yourself a good deal of time, frustration, and futile effort. Here are a few examples of initial "blunt statement" introductions:

> ❯ In this paper, I intend to show that Van Dusen's analysis of civil disobedience is unbalanced.

> ❯ I want to argue that the legalization of drugs constitutes a kind of false progress that will result in an American culture that is even worse off than it is at present under the admittedly-flawed policies of criminalization.

> ❯ In this paper, I intend to argue that the redistribution of wealth to underdeveloped nations would permit better management of most major threats to international security.

> ❯ In my rebuttal to the Bethe chapter's resolution, I want to suggest that passive euthanasia is a cop-out that simply lets us avoid confronting the difficult issues raised by death in a high-tech society.

> ❯ In analyzing the *Los Angeles Times* as a cultural artifact, I would like to point out that it conveys the distinct impression that, as a culture, we are all bit actors in a low budget techno-thriller written by someone with the intellectual range of a car alarm—everything is violence and graduated threats.

"Funnel" Introductions

This is a standard but quite reliable and effective method of introduction. The introductory paragraph begins with a fairly broad discussion of the background information the reader will need to have to understand the author's position. This **background material** usually includes the topic and issue under discussion, and it may also include important terminology or information that the paper will depend upon or frequently refer to. Once the background information is presented, the introduction narrows or "funnels" to the author's specific thesis. The sequence of background information before the thesis reflects an important understanding of the reader's perspective on the essay. Without the preparatory framework of background information, the reader is unlikely to grasp the significance of the thesis. Moreover, if the thesis is presented before the framing information, then the reader's understanding of the thesis is likely to be blurred by the background material. Finally, by placing the thesis at the end of the introduction one has a much easier time setting up a transition to the argument of the first body paragraph. For example:

> No one who reads the newspaper or who has any contact with daily life in our cities can doubt the accuracy of Mike Royko's recent claim that America has lost the war on drugs (559). On the foreign fronts, the high-tech and highly-touted efforts to interdict the drug flow from producer nations have had little effect in reducing drug supply. On the home front, the situation is little better. While education programs may have helped to reduce the recent wave of crack addiction, drug use remains high and drug crime seems to be increasing. Because of these defeats, Royko and other commentators such as Michael S. Gazzaniga advocate the legalization of drugs as our one remaining hope. Although I recognize and share Royko's and Gazzaniga's frustration over the difficulty of controlling illegal drugs, I cannot concur with their proposal. While they seem to offer a progressive solution to the drug impasse, I believe that the progress promised by drug legalization is largely illusionary and would result in an American culture that is even worse off than it is today.

Anecdotal Introductions

This type of introduction, one often seen in journalistic writing, uses a two-part approach: a concrete example or "representative anecdote" of the point to be discussed is followed by a more conventional presentation of the issue and the author's main line of argument. Consider the following example:

> It was always interesting to watch whenever the Criminal Intelligence Division (CID) raided one of the barracks on our base in Germany. "El Cid," as the narcs were affectionately called, used dogs to nose out the hashish that was then the troops' drug of choice, and as soon as the dogs entered the building a hail of hash pipes, stash bags, and smoking paraphernalia would begin to rain down from the upper windows. The CID made quick progress with their searches and soon the dopers among us had switched from hashish to heroin—a drug the dogs had much more difficulty detecting. Of course, this progress entailed a somewhat paradoxical and perhaps unforeseeable consequence: rather than having a number of slightly stoned hash users we now had a smaller number of heroin addicts who were not only more seriously debilitated but who sometimes wound up dead from overdoses.
>
> The point of this little morality tale is not, as it may seem, to underscore the futility of drug control and thus to advocate the legalization of drugs as a means of improving American culture. While I recognize that our current approaches to drug control are only slightly less inept than those of the CID dog patrols, I do not believe that the ineffectiveness of drug

criminalization can be used to argue the potential effectiveness of drug legalization. My point has rather to do with what the CID agents and advocates of drug legalization have in common: a blind and self-confident faith that what they are doing represents progress. In my opinion, the legalization of drugs stands as an ideal of false progress that is likely only to worsen the problems facing our culture.

Concealed-Thesis Introductions

These are often used when addressing a hostile audience that might stop listening to your argument if you were to announce your thesis initially. The trick here is to provide a *main direction* for your paper, one that will allow you to control your argument and let you lead the audience more gradually to your position. Your thesis will thus need to be reserved until fairly late in your text.

The following sample introductory paragraph is written to an audience that favors drug legalization by an author who, while recognizing some merit in that position, actually does not favor it as a principal response to the drug crisis. To avoid losing the audience before having an opportunity to persuade them to modify their position, the author uses an introductory approach that proposes a main line of analysis for the paper to follow, rather than a thesis definitely stating the author's position. Notice how the introductory paragraph criticizes policies of drug criminalization, speaks respectfully of proposals for drug legalization, and funnels to a simple proposal—in lieu of a thesis statement revealing the author's actual stance—that legalization deserves careful and impartial analysis (which the author then would undertake in the body of the paper):

> ❯ Virtually no one disputes the human and cultural devastation caused by the sale and use of illegal drugs. However, most Americans seem almost defiantly unwilling to consider alternatives to policies of criminalization and incarceration that over the last forty years have done almost nothing to reduce, let along eliminate, the scourge of the illicit drug trade from American society. Does this make sense? Decade after decade and administration after administration, the theme of criminalization has been to "get tough on drugs," yet no matter how fast we build and fill prisons, we find ourselves incapable of diminishing drug trafficking, to the point that today lesser offenders are being released upon conviction simply for lack of jail space. Given the manifest failure of drug criminalization, one might imagine that at least some attention would be given to alternative responses to the drug problem, and that chief among these would be the legalization of a significant range of drugs now on the registry of illicit substances. Unfortunately, drug legalization is seldom given close and serious consideration, but is instead ignored or dismissed as an impossibly idealistic proposal that is both soft-hearted and soft-headed. I believe that such dismissiveness is not only unwise but intellectually narrow-minded. While I do not claim that legalization represents a panacea for the drug crisis, I do believe that it merits a careful and honest analysis of both its strengths and its potential drawbacks as a central policy of drug control.

The following paragraph, finally giving the author's stance or thesis, would come after the body of paper has argued that certain features of drug legalization have utility in the struggle against drug culture, but that large-scale legalization represents a form of false progress likely to backfire. Depending upon circumstances, such a paragraph might serve as a conclusion, or as a "pivot" into further development of the author's thesis.

> ❯ Thus I would suggest that while drug legalization points the way to a resolution of the drug crisis in American society, it does not represent a policy that can at this time wisely or safely be adopted as a principal large-scale response to the problems of drug abuse. As I have tried to show in my analysis, legalization or decriminalization reflects a progressive approach that

may well succeed within the very specific context of relatively small and placid communities of users involved with less addictive substances. Unfortunately, the present drug crisis has moved almost entirely beyond this context, and now involves exceptionally addictive drugs and violent forms of national and international narco-trafficking and (increasingly) narco-terrorism, all of which raise economic issues and security concerns that legalization simply cannot handle. Despite this, however, I nonetheless believe that those committed to legalization are entirely correct with regard to the two central points motivating their argument: that the drug culture will remain impervious to solutions based on criminalization and incarceration, and that our best hope resides in undertaking profound social reforms that will provide the grounds for more meaningful and fulfilling lives—both economically and spiritually—for all Americans. Any effective response to the drug crisis will need to take account of both these realizations.

Other Ways to Start

Here are some additional introductory tactics—each with advantages and disadvantages—that you might consider using in conjunction with the approaches described above.

Bold Statement/Lead with Thesis

"Given the breathtaking pace of the development of genetic engineering, the government has no choice but to restrict and closely regulate the use of this technology in our agriculture industries."

"Only fools try to stop the march of technology, and the safe growth of the biotechnology industry proves that the government should not impose further restrictions on this important sector of our economy."

Advantages	*Disadvantages*
❭ Helps to immediately narrow your topic	❭ Without a strong thesis the statement will seem obvious and trivial
❭ Engages your reader right away	❭ What else can you say in intro? Avoid repetition of thesis—focus instead on previewing arguments
❭ Argue from strength	
❭ Thesis quickly recognized and easily referred to	

Reframe or Narrow the Question

"The development and use of genetic technology raises many difficult technical questions that often baffle non-scientists. Instead of leaving the issue to a professional clique, however, let's begin with the most fundamental question: is biotechnology really different than other human advances? Specifically, do the standards traditionally applied to scientific innovations adequately cover the challenges of genetic engineering?"

Advantages

> Effective narrowing technique

> Authoritative ("I know the real question")

> The structure of the essay can be encoded in the way you rephrase the question

Disadvantages

> If you take too long you'll lose your reader (i.e., to be authoritative you have to be clear and concise)

> *Not* a substitute for a clear and direct thesis—eventually your essay has to answer the "new" question

Define the Opposition

"Advances in biotechnology have forced scientists, politicians and religious leaders alike to grapple with questions concerning the extent to which the natural development of a human life can be altered. Hidden between the lines of the rhetoric of medical advances, however, lurks a dangerous return to eugenics and the development of a new 'master race.' For those who applaud the use of genetic engineering in fighting diseases, it is a short step to begin planning the 'perfect' human."

Advantages

> Specific target

> Keeps you focused

> Continue to refer to opposition throughout paper

Disadvantages

> Too harsh and you'll lose credibility

> Be specific in naming opposition—vagueness hurts credibility

> Eventually you need to give positive reasons for your position

> *Not* a substitute for a clear and direct thesis—trashing someone isn't an argument

Quote

"While there are many concerns to be addressed in the use of genetic engineering in our agriculture industries, fears that we are somehow 'tampering' with nature are unfounded. As the editors of *The New Republic* asserted in a May 23, 1988 editorial, '[w]e long ago decided that sacrificing animals to science, and to our appetites, is justified.' They add that we also have a long history of *creating* animals for our use—citing the breeding of dogs, pigs and horses as examples" (507–08).

Advantages

> Authority of source transferred to you

> Quote can help to reframe question (see above) or establish opposition (see above)

> Nature of source can set context for the debate and establish audience (e.g., newspaper editorial, academic paper, etc.)

Disadvantages

> Must be an effective and concise statement or else you'll lose your reader

> Quote must be explained within the context of your paper

> *Not* a substitute for a clear and direct thesis—only you can state your opinions

Hard Facts

"In 1986, *The New York Times* reported that each year 390,000 American workers contract disabling occupational illnesses (various cancers, anemias, dermatitis, asthma, emphysema, etc.) and that 100,000 die annually from these diseases (Hunt 473). Still, these startling figures do not provide justification for the increasing use of genetic screening by American industries."

Advantages	*Disadvantages*
❯ Credibility from source	❯ If facts are wrong, or even sound wrong, credibility is lost
❯ Demonstrates urgency or timeliness of the debate	❯ Too many facts and reader is bored
❯ Sounds smart	❯ *Not* a substitute for a clear and direct thesis—facts are not enough to make a strong argument

Short Narrative

"My father was a diabetic for the last twenty-five years of his life. Twice a day he received an insulin shot that helped to maintain his blood sugar. Although this treatment extended his life, he feared the side-effects (damaged eyesight, poor circulation, loss of limbs, etc.) from using cow insulin, the only inexpensive and readily available source. The development of genetically engineered human insulin in the early eighties took much of the fear out of the last years of my father's life, and is just one example of the many ways in which biotechnology can help afflicted individuals. Today, we are on the verge of an era in which diseases like diabetes can be avoided even before a child is born. Despite the objections of short-sighted individuals, no restrictions should be placed on genetic engineering."

Advantages	*Disadvantages*
❯ Engaging and personal; it draws reader in	❯ If it's too long or off-topic it will bore your reader and you'll lose credibility
❯ Connection with "real life" (this approach is very popular in newspapers now)	❯ Needs a clear and obvious connection with topic
	❯ NOT a substitute for a clear and direct thesis—your opinions should back up your story (why should someone care unless it's connected)

Metaphor, Symbol, or Reference

"In their enthusiasm for genetic engineering, scientists have presented the American public with what amounts to a Trojan horse. Bottom-line businesses and heartless insurance companies wait within to use biotechnology to further erode our freedoms and invade our privacy."

"In his classic novel *Brave New World,* Aldous Huxley presents a frightening image of a society in which human are genetically programmed. Are we headed for that future?"

Advantages	*Disadvantages*
❯ Quickly narrows	❯ Reference should be obvious
❯ Lends credibility	❯ Must be quick—it's your paper, not Huxley's novel
❯ Can return to metaphor, etc., throughout the paper—helps with transitions and overall structure (the "glue" of an essay)	

Early Drafting Practices

Drafting is that stage of the writing process that most closely resembles what people commonly think of as writing: the production of text in sentences and paragraphs. Yet it is important to keep in mind that drafting is recursively linked to both prewriting and revision. Not only will your draft follow the guidelines laid down in the rough plan you produced as part of your prewriting, but you may also find yourself breaking away from your draft to do additional invention and planning. Similarly, your draft not only provides the foundation for later revisions but also will itself involve revision; first drafts, for example, are never completed without striking out words and deleting, shifting, or modifying sentences. For all this, however, drafting remains an identifiable stage in the writing process, the place where you first have to confront the blank page and begin the difficult task of transforming the free and satisfying nebulousness of thought into the twisty and resistant medium of language.

Because drafting is challenging, the following drafting practices are suggested for your consideration. Please note that some of them offer advice that is apparently contradictory (e.g., keeping your plan in mind even while expecting your ideas to evolve). This merely reflects the fact that writing, because it is a complex activity, cannot be defined by a discrete set of rules but always requires judgment on the writer's part to select the proper course of action depending upon context and circumstances.

Don't procrastinate. The more you delay beginning a draft, the harder it becomes to begin. The longer you take in completing your draft, the less time you will have to revise it. A substantial percentage of students prevent themselves from writing to their full potential because they wait until the last day or two to actually begin writing. Don't be one of them.

Starting is miserable. The reason many people procrastinate when it comes to drafting is that starting is almost always an ugly struggle. In a way, drafting is like running: until you establish a rhythm, nothing feels right, but the only way to find your rhythm is to start moving and tough it out. You may be able to reduce the strain, however, by finding a way to "warm up" beforehand. When Steinbeck was writing *East of Eden,* for example, he was said to have begun each day's work by writing a letter to a friend. Just be careful that your warm-up activities don't become rituals of avoidance.

Don't let your introduction stop you. Introductions are meant to begin things for the reader, but they can have an unfortunate tendency to stop things for the writer. A first draft doesn't even need an introduction; it is simply a coherent sequence of body paragraphs that advances your provisional thesis or main line of argument. If you find yourself re-doing drafts of your introduction rather than generating drafts of body paragraphs, just let the introduction go. You can return to it during revision, when you will have a better sense of your overall text and will thus be better prepared to introduce it. Indeed, many writers don't even attempt to draft an introduction until they have completed a draft of the body of the paper.

Be messy. Like prewriting, drafting *should* be messy. Your purpose is to get down your ideas in rough form for later revision, *not* to produce something approaching a finished draft. When drafting, keep moving and ignore small problems. Don't stop to correct misspellings; they're much easier to catch with your spell checker after everything is fully revised. Don't stop to rearrange a sentence if it is simpler just to follow it with a second version, deleting the first version when you revise the paragraph.

Be organized. While you shouldn't worry about the messiness of your draft, you do want to retain an image of the architecture of your proposed paper and a sense of what the paragraph you're working on is *doing* and how it relates to the paragraph ahead of it and to the one that will follow. One way to do this is to keep your rough plan in mind; another is to use a preceding paragraph to launch you into the one that will follow. Before working on a new paragraph, read the previous one aloud to remind yourself what you were arguing and to set up your transition into the next paragraph.

Keep the assignment and your plan in mind. Once you begin drafting, it's surprisingly easy to forget what you're doing and to write your way straight off topic. This can be avoided by referring frequently to your rough plan and occasionally back to the assignment sheet itself. Another traditional piece of advice is to write your thesis on a small card and pin this up directly in front of you, so that you will see it whenever you raise your head.

Expect your prewriting ideas to evolve. *All* writing is creative writing, and the creative process does not end when you complete the rough plan for your paper. You should therefore anticipate that your thinking will shift as you begin drafting your paper, and in fact will continue to evolve as you revise it. This is a good thing, since it will allow you to sharpen your argument or deepen your analysis. The only time you need to be careful is when new ideas start to pull you off topic or undermine the coherence of your draft. If new concepts evolve from your initial ideas, you should be able to work them into your draft, but sometimes they seem to call for an entirely different approach and thus a new paper. In such cases, you need to consider whether the new argument is actually superior or just greener grass *and* whether enough time remains for you to start over and still make your deadline.

Don't get stalled. In writing your first draft, you'll often find yourself having a hard time articulating a particularly challenging idea or argument. If you get stuck on such a paragraph, try moving beyond it to finish up the remainder of your draft. When you later return to the conceptual obstacle, you may find that having better command of your overall argument makes it easier to complete the paragraph.

Of course, there may times when you simply can't advance without first working through a perplexing concept, and in such instances you simply have to hammer away at the problem until you straighten it out. Keep in mind, however, that such cases are sometimes better addressed by temporarily abandoning the attempt to draft the paragraph in order to return to invention activities that will help you reconceptualize your basic idea or argument.

Save fancy for later. You can make your language elegant and your arguments refined during revision, but first you have to get there, and that's the purpose of drafting. Don't worry if your first draft sounds awkward or strained; simply get it down. Be direct and plain. If you find yourself hung up about what to say, just write "What I want to say in this paragraph is that _____" and fill in the blank using the simplest possible language.

Specialized Paragraphs: Conclusions

A conclusion should, as the word implies, bring your argument to a satisfying close. It should point backwards, reminding your reader of your thesis (usually one sentence will do), but more importantly, it should point forwards, into the future. Once you've constructed a strong argument, you've earned the right to point the audience toward solutions and new directions for research. You might thus try to answer some of the following questions: What should the reader do now? Where does this leave us? Can you suggest a call to action?

Some "don'ts":

> Don't restate each of your points/topic sentences. If during revisions you notice that you have created a complete summary of your paper, consider recycling this writing back into your body paragraphs. Often summary conclusions will offer clearer writing and a better assessment of what each paragraph was actually about. Move such valuable writing up to form stronger claims the first time they are made.

> Don't introduce a brand new example or point. The conclusion is the place to rest your case and look for an exit.

Some "do's":

> Restate your thesis once in order to give a satisfying sense of closure.

> Point out some provocative implications of your thesis. Answer questions like "What now?" or "What's the significance of what I've said?"

> Can you return to touch briefly on your introduction's "hook" or anecdote to provide a satisfying frame to your essay?

> What question has your essay answered? Why is it important?

> What would make a reader regret coming to the end of such a satisfying essay? Seek to put the audience in the proper mood, or provide a stylistic flourish to signal you've reached the close of the argument. As in the introduction, the conclusion can be a good place for appeals to emotion and figurative language (pathos).

Examples. Review the following samples from published works to assess the way these writers provide a purposeful and well-planned ending for their essays.

From Susan Bordo "The Globalization of Eating Disorders"

> What is to be done? I have no easy answers. But I do know that we need to acknowledge, finally and decisively, that we are dealing here with a cultural problem. If eating disorders were bio-chemical, as some claim, how can we account for their gradual "spread" across race, gender and nationality? And with mass media culture increasingly providing the dominant "public education" in our children's lives—and those of children around the globe—how can we blame families? Families matter, of course, and so do racial and ethnic traditions. But the families exist in cultural time and space—and so do racial groups. In the empire of images, no one lives in a bubble of self-generated "dysfunction" or permanent immunity. The sooner we recognize that—and start paying attention to the culture around us and what it is teaching our children—the sooner we can begin developing some strategies for change.

From Bill Gates "Saving the World is Within Our Grasp"

> I believe we stand at a moment of unequaled opportunity. Governments must now step up to the plate with more money—wisely targeted—to expand effective global health programs to reach all those in need. Businesses, community groups and individuals all play a role as well. When Melinda and I visited that PEPFAR clinic in South Africa, we were thrilled to see the progress we've made against one deadly disease. I'm now more convinced than ever that we can create a healthier world for everyone.

From Marc Lappe and Britt Baily "Biotechnology's Negative Impact on World Agriculture"

> We are thus left with disturbing questions as transgenic crops go into mass production. How much are we willing to jeopardize the evolutionary future of our food crops? How much uncertainty is generated by transgenic creation of new plants? And are we really ready to let large corporations play God in the critical area of food biotechnology?

From Roger Scrunton "A Carnivore's Credo"

> I would suggest that it is not only permissible for those who care about animals to eat meat; they have a duty to do so. If meat eating should ever be confined to those who do not care about animal suffering, then compassionate farming would cease. Where there are conscientious carnivores, there is a motive to raise animals kindly. Moreover, conscientious carnivores show their depraved contemporaries that there is a right and wrong way to eat. Duty requires us, therefore, to eat our friends.

Review the following samples from student work to determine the qualities that make for a satisfying conclusion. Do they summarize? Point to broader implications? Answer the "so what" questions? Employ stylistic flourish? What else?

1. The Wilderness Act has been able to effectively prevent the encroachment of humanity on wilderness areas for the last half-century. It has shown that we must continue to guard our wilderness areas. More importantly, it has shown that people must take action to preserve natural areas for future generations. Nature can balance itself out, but people must help it. Invasive species have to be confronted head on and neutralized before they can cause more damage than they have already. Low-intensity wildfires need to be allowed to periodically burn areas that would burn naturally, so they do not turn into infernos that destroy everything in their path. There needs to be recognition of the role that hunters and fisherman play in

controlling animal populations. Funding to restore areas that have come under cultivation needs to be secured. Finally, people need to recognize the role that they must play to ensure that the solutions to these problems are implemented, not forgotten. Wilderness means a lot to American History. The promise of building a life in the wilderness was the first American dream. It is part of America's national identity. If the American people fail to preserve the wilderness, then they will fail to preserve a cornerstone of their heritage.

2. When the Wilderness Act materialized fifty years ago, its proponents could not have predicted the state of the environment today, just as we cannot predict the state of the environment fifty years from today. We can only hope, like our ancestors, that our actions will prevent the extinction of both the wilderness and our species. Let us not waste any more time arguing over the value of nature or the justification for intervention; humanity is simply too invested in nature to let it decay any further. Stabilizing the wilderness will ultimately ensure its survival and strengthen our connection to nature, but we can only achieve this goal by becoming gardeners. So, we will be gardeners, and the wilderness will become our bountiful garden, capable of producing whatever fruits we will it to bear. Only then can we truly flourish.

**Do's and don'ts adapted from Kennedy, X. J.; Kennedy, Dorothy M.; Muth, Marcia F. *Writing and Revising: A Portable Guide*. Boston: Bedford/St. Martin's, 2007.

Style

Fundamental Syntactic Considerations

Active/Passive Constructions

In many (but not all) contexts, English word order favors placing the doer (or agent) of an action in the subject position of a sentence, ahead of the verb (which names the action) and of the object (which names what was "done-to"). Sentences that place the agent of an action in the position of the grammatical subject are called active:

Active: The horse pulled the cart.

For a variety of reasons—some good, some less so—this order is often reversed, with whatever was "done-to" being moved to the front of the sentence as the grammatical subject and the agent being moved to the end of the sentence. Sentences of this type, which put the cart before the horse, are called passive:

Passive: The cart was pulled by the horse.

Sometimes a passive sentence will drop any reference to the agent who did the action. This kind of sentence is known as an agentless passive:

Agentless Passive: The cart was pulled.

In English, the active form of a sentence is generally clearer, cleaner, and more direct than the passive form. Passive sentences waste words and sometimes confuse the subject-agent relationship.

Postponed subject constructions compound the weaknesses of the passive, since they add even more words and insert a place-holding pronoun (an *it* or *there*) as the grammatical subject:

Postponed Subject (Active):   There was a horse that pulled the cart.

Postponed Subject (Passive):   There was a cart that was pulled by a horse.

Postponed subject sentences are easy to identify and revise: simply delete the initial *it is, there is, there are,* etc., and then cut out whatever relative pronoun (*that, which, who,* etc.) has been embedded in the underlying active or passive sentence:

~~There was~~ a horse ~~that~~ pulled the cart.

Note, however, that passive constructions are useful when you wish to place emphasis not on the agent but on the quality or object of his or her actions, and they may be required in other instances as well: "The man was murdered" (if you don't know by whom). But passive sentences may conceal the issue of who did what to whom. Compare the following:

> I shot the sheriff, but I did not shoot the deputy. *(Active version)*

> The sheriff was shot by me, but the deputy was not shot by me. *(Passive version)*

> I emphatically and indignantly deny shooting the deputy. It may possibly be true, however, that the sheriff was tragically struck down by a projectile issuing from a weapon that was held by a hand that was attached—merely through the accident of birth—to an arm that belongs to me. *(Lawyer's version)*

Unless you *intend* to conceal responsibility, use the active form.

Parallel Structure

The concept of **parallel structure** provides one of the most important techniques for making sentences not only tighter but also more forceful. While parallel structure may be used to fashion complex and sophisticated sentences, the concept itself is quite simple. In essence, parallel structure simply combines in one sentence those sections that might otherwise be stated in two or more sentences of the same (thus parallel) form. For example, the sentence *I like apples, peaches, and pears* may be understood as a conflation of three precursive sentences:

> *I like apples.*

> *I like peaches.*

> *I like pears.*

The advantage of using a single sentence with parallel structure here is obvious, for the triple repetition of *I like* is entirely unnecessary.

Parallel structure always involves a "trunk-and-branch" arrangement, and for parallel structure sentences to work effectively, the branch elements should be of exactly the same grammatical form. Consider the following incorrect example:

> We went to the market, to the bookstore, and saw a movie. *(error)*

Here the trunk is *We went*, and the first two branches fit it exactly: *We went to the market* and *We went to the bookstore*. Notice, however, that the third branch doesn't fit onto the trunk: *We went saw a movie* (error). It's usually possible to revise such non-parallel structures without too much difficulty:

> We went to the market, to the bookstore, and to the movies.

In some cases, each branch may fit the trunk, but the parallel structure will still be thrown off by mismatches between the branches themselves. In the following modification of the first example, for instance, the structure is no longer precisely parallel:

> I like apples, peaches, and eating pears. *(error)*

Almost any sentence element can be used as the branching element in creating parallel structure, and complete sentences can themselves be placed into parallel relationships. In the following example, four sentences are combined into a single parallel structure. Notice that the fourth sentence contains an additional parallel structure of its own.

> Stock values plummeted, commodity prices collapsed, banks failed, and millions of people lost their jobs, their savings, their homes, and their hopes.

Because parallel structure provides such an effective method for tightening loose prose, it's useful to be aware of the many possible ways in which it may be employed. Familiarity with the following examples may sharpen your eye as you read through and revise your own writing.

Subjects: *Clerks, bailiffs, and court recorders* were all affected by the regulation, although lawyers were not.

Verbs: He *argued, pleaded,* and *threatened*, but to no avail.

Verbs with objects: As soon as the telescope arrived, they quickly *leveled the mount, collimated the optical components,* and *aligned the polar axis.*

Objects: The hydraulic leak threatened the *flaps, ailerons,* and *brakes.*

Adjectives: A series of *brief, clear, pointless* communiqués did little to reduce growing diplomatic tensions.

Infinitives: The epitaph, drawn from Tennyson, spoke of their commitment *"to strive, to seek, to find, and not to yield."*

Prepositional Phrases: "...that government *of the people, by the people, for the people,* shall not perish from the earth."

Gerund Phrases: In summer they enjoyed *climbing the cliffs, fishing the streams, and exploring the woods.*

Participial Phrases: *Belching smoke and puffing steam,* an old coal-burning switch engine shoved a line of freight cars together at one end of the marshalling yard.

Sentence Conflation

The same tactic used to create parallel structure sentences—combining parts of several sentences within a single sentence—may be used even when the precursive sentences are not parallel. In the example that follows, a core sentence is repeatedly modified by adding various elements from different precursive sentences. In the first example, for instance, the precursive sentence must have been something similar to *Mary was a unicycle champion*. By "conflating" sentences is this way you are able to increase the force of your writing while eliminating unnecessary words and phrases.

Core Sentence: Mary joined the Foreign Legion.

Modifications:

1. Mary, a unicycle champion, joined the Foreign Legion.

2a. Mary, sensitive and refined, joined the Foreign Legion.
    Mary, intelligent but bored, joined the Foreign Legion.

2b. Mary, brilliant in many ways, joined the Foreign Legion.

3. Feeling the need for a change, Mary joined the Foreign Legion.

4a. Because she needed the money, Mary joined the Foreign Legion.

4b. Mary, who needed the money, joined the Foreign Legion.

5. Mary, in France for a vacation, joined the Foreign Legion.

6. Her life at a standstill, Mary joined the Foreign Legion.
    The circus having folded, Mary joined the Foreign Legion.
    Her parents being absent, Mary joined the Foreign Legion.

7a. Mary joined the Foreign Legion, a unit known for its traditions.

7b. Mary dated Jean-Paul and Albert, legionnaires in her company.

Stylistic Devices

A stylistic device is a sentence form that is "re-useable": the same underlying structure can be employed in completely different contexts to create completely different assertions. The more stylistic devices you have at your command, the more options you will have as a writer. By keeping an eye out for such devices in your daily reading and by recording one or two in your journal, you can quickly build up a sizeable collection and, at the same time, improve your own abilities in terms of surface-level revision.

For each device, copy the sentence you wish to imitate, underlining those parts that make up the stylistic device you have identified. Then construct a schematic diagram of the device, underlining the stable parts of the form and using an "X" or "Y" to represent variable content (see examples, below). Finally, imitate the form, providing new and different content of your own, and once again underlining the stable parts of the form. Provide a short source citation for each device.

In selecting stylistic devices to imitate, keep in mind three things:

—choose a form that can be applied in a wide variety of contexts;

—choose a form that you already recognize and understand but that you don't presently use;

—choose a form that you think would be helpful to your writing.

Sample Stylistic Devices

The following examples address the topic of changing family values and structures.

1. a. <u>When</u> King's heirs devote themselves to building a virtual civil-rights march, <u>how long before</u> we learn to content ourselves with virtual rights? (Henry Louis Gates, Jr., "Heroes, Inc." The *New Yorker*, Jan. 16, 1995.)

    b. Form: <u>When</u> X, <u>how long before</u> Y?

    c. Imitation: <u>When</u> competition begins to dominate the life of a culture, <u>how long before</u> it begins to dominate the life of the family?

2. a <u>The</u> construction of heroes <u>becomes the</u> deconstruction of heroism.... (Gates, ibid.)

    b. Form: <u>The</u> X <u>becomes the</u> OPPOSITE-X.

    c. Imitation: <u>The</u> triumph of materialistic values <u>leads to the</u> humiliation of family values. (Notice slight modification of form.)

3. a. <u>But, as always in</u> history, what is forgotten is as crucial as what is remembered. (Gates, ibid.)

    b. Form: <u>But, as always in</u> X, Y.

    c. Imitation: <u>But, as always in</u> dealing with complex issues, we need to consider whether simple solutions are likely to be effective or merely attractive.

4. a. Simplify, simplify—<u>that is the</u> imperative of the hero industry. (Gates, ibid.)

    b. Form: X, X—<u>that is the</u> Y.

    c. Imitation: Working mothers, working mothers—<u>that is the</u> constant refrain of those who trace all family problems back to the demise of the traditional patriarchal family.

5. a. <u>It used to be said that</u> we got the heroes we deserved. <u>Times have changed: today</u> we get the heroes we manufacture. (Gates, ibid.)

    b. Form: <u>It used to be said that</u> X. <u>Times have changed: today</u> Y.

    c. Imitation: <u>It used to be said that</u> the family had only one form. <u>Times have changed: today</u> it seems that the family can take any form.

6. a. <u>Each saw</u> the projection of his own image <u>as central to</u> the success or failure of his broader political program. (Gates, ibid.)

    b. Form: <u>Each saw</u> X <u>as central to</u> Y.

    c. Imitation: <u>Each sees</u> economic factors <u>as central to</u> the problems presently facing American families. (Notice slight modification of form.)

7. a. I look around for the girls, but they're gone, <u>of course</u>. (John Updike, "A & P," *Little Brown Reader*, 387.)

    b. Form: X, <u>of course</u>.

    c. Imitation: Those who most insist upon a return to the traditional family structure do not, <u>of course</u>, want to change the economic conditions that make such a return impossible. (Notice modification: insertion is shifted from final position to middle position.)

8. a. Lengel sighs and begins to look very patient <u>and</u> old <u>and</u> gray. (Updike, ibid.)

   b. Form: X <u>and</u> Y <u>and</u> Z.

   c. Imitation: Genuine human development requires time <u>and</u> patience <u>and</u> trust.

9. a. "We *<u>are</u>* decent," Queenie says suddenly. . . .

   b. Form: X *<u>is/are</u>* Y. (Italics or underlining for emphasis.)

   c. Imitation: The family *<u>is</u>* still necessary, but it cannot continue in its traditional form.

10. a. <u>The longer</u> her neck was, <u>the more</u> of her there was. (Updike, ibid.)

    b. Form: <u>The longer</u> X, <u>the more</u> Y.

    c. Imitation: <u>The longer</u> we take to address the needs of the family, <u>the more</u> our society will decay.

Commonplace Entries

A commonplace entry is simply a passage of writing that is copied down in a journal to save as an example of style or as a nugget of wisdom or a piece of useful information—something that one may wish to memorize for future use. The stylistic devices described above may be considered as very brief commonplace entries, which more usually run to a paragraph or more in length. Commonplace entries not only provide a good way to expand your vocabulary and syntactic range but they may also serve as an excellent means of study. By keeping commonplace entries relevant to the discipline that you are studying, you can become familiar with important ideas while at the same time developing an understanding for the discourse conventions and style appropriate to the discipline.

Commonplace entries may also provide a basis for exercises in stylistic imitation. To practice stylistic imitation, select one of the following passages and read it over two or three times. Ask yourself what characterizes the style of the passage and how that style compares with that of the other passages. Work toward a sense of the form of the passage—the function words, rhythms, and sentence "moves" that constitute a stable and replicable structure for the "content" of the passage. (A good way to do this is with a schematic diagram similar to that used above with the stylistic devices.)

Once you have a good sense of how the passage is structured, think of a topic that is entirely different than that discussed in the passage, one that will afford a different "content" for its form. Using this new topic, write an imitation of the passage, doing the best you can to capture its style and structure.

> To be at the center of things, to know people who disposed of enormous power, who could take certain graces and prerogatives for granted, to mingle with the decorative and decorated world, to hear the butler announce a name that was old when Shakespeare was alive, these were things to which she could never be wholly indifferent.
>
> —Quentin Bell, *Virginia Woolf*

> Her eyes had been going in and out among the curves and shadows of the fruit, among the rich purples of the lowland grapes, then over the horny ridge of the shell, putting a yellow against a purple, a curved shape against a round shape, without knowing why she did it, or why, every time she did it, she felt more and more serene; until, oh what a pity that they should do it—a hand reached out, took a pear, and spoilt the whole thing.
>
> —Virginia Woolf, *To the Lighthouse*

In the late summer of that year we lived in a house in a village that looked across the river and the plain to the mountains. In the bed of the river there were pebbles and boulders, dry and white in the sun, and the water was clear and swiftly moving and blue in the channels. Troops went by the house and down the road and the dust they raised powdered the leaves of the trees. The trunks of the trees too were dusty and the leaves fell early that year and we saw the troops marching along the road and the dust rising and leaves, stirred by the breeze, falling and the soldiers marching and afterward the road bare and white except for the leaves.

—Ernest Hemingway, *A Farewell to Arms*

He stepped into the stream. It was a shock. His trousers clung tight to his legs. His shoes felt the gravel. The water was a rising cold shock.

———————

In the pack he found a big onion. He sliced it in two and peeled the silky outer skin. Then he cut one half into slices and made onion sandwiches. He wrapped them in oiled paper and buttoned them in the other pocket of his khaki shirt. He turned the skillet upside down on the grill, drank the coffee, sweetened and yellow brown with the condensed milk in it, and tidied up the camp. It was a good camp.

—Ernest Hemingway, "Big Two-Hearted River"

I imagined victims for those wolves, I made
them phantoms to follow.
They have hunted the phantoms and missed the house. It is not
good to forget over what gulfs the spirit
Of the beauty of humanity, the petal of a lost flower blown
seaward by the night-wind, floats to its quietness.

—Robinson Jeffers, "Apology for Bad Dreams"

Quotation Tactics

Using Direct Quotation

Quoting a passage means copying a passage exactly as it appears in a source and incorporating it into your essay, and students often find it tempting to use numerous direct quotations because this is easier to do than paraphrasing or summarizing. Do not give in to this temptation, though; use direct quotations only when you have a good reason for doing so. If the author is an acknowledged expert or authority in the field, you may wish to use his or her words exactly. In this case, be sure to indicate the nature of this expertise within your text. Here is an example:

> Dr. John Salinger, Director of the Johnson Institute for the Study of Canine Behavior, claims that "dogs have been domesticated for many thousands of years longer than had been previously believed."

Other reasons for using direct quotation include instances in which the person being quoted said something remarkably well or when the quotation would lend strength to your essay that would be lost in a paraphrase or summary. Be careful about too many quotations, though. You want your essay to reflect your own ideas and personal style, not to consist of a series of quotations all strung together.

Supporting Quotations

Quotations are most commonly used to *support* a point or claim that you, as author, wish to make. Notice that this implies a corollary idea—that quotations should *not* be used in places where they might replace your own assertions, such as in the thesis statement or in topic sentences.

In setting up a supporting quotation, you need to ensure that:

> ❯ the point you are making is clear, and

> ❯ the relationship of the quotation to this point is also apparent.

Compare the following two passages, which use quotations from Dr. Martin Luther King, Jr.'s "Letter from Birmingham Jail" (1963). Dr. King composed this letter after being arrested for participating in coordinated marches and sit-ins against racial segregation in Birmingham, Alabama. While in jail, Dr. King read a newspaper article written by eight white Alabama clergymen, critiquing King for his nonviolent methods of resistance. Provoked in particular by the clergymen's insistence that racial segregation should be fought in the courts rather than in the streets, Dr. King defended nonviolent resistance on legal, political, and historical grounds. The quotations directly cited here provide some of the reasoning for King's defense of nonviolence:

1. King was not an extremist. As he said of himself, "I have tried to stand between these two forces, saying that we need emulate neither the 'do-nothingism' of the complacent nor the hatred and despair of the black nationalist" (508). King argues that oppressed people need some kind of outlet. "If his repressed emotions are not released in nonviolent ways, they will seek expression through violence" (509). Instead King chose non-violence, "and now this approach is being termed extremist" (509).

2. It is both inaccurate and unfair to accuse King of extremism. King clearly thought of himself as a moderate, as one who chose to stand between what he termed the "opposing forces" of "complacency" on the one hand and of "bitterness and hatred" on the other (508). Thus King explicitly rejected both the "'do-nothingism' of the complacent" and the "hatred and despair of the black nationalist," arguing instead for "the more excellent way of love and non-violent protest" (508). Of course, King's non-violent opposition may be made to *appear* extreme when viewed from the skewed perspective of Van Dusen's complacent disregard for the evils King opposed, but I would argue that King's position is in fact the more moderate. Complacency in the presence of oppression is a kind of passive and covert extremism, one that seems sedate and refined yet one that is finally complicit with more active and overt forms of extremism because it serves to nurture the conditions that inevitably explode in exactly that violence which the complacent so piously decry. In pointing out that "[w]e will have to repent in this generation not merely for the hateful words and actions of the bad people but for the appalling silence of the good people" (507), King reminds us that genuine moderation cannot consist of silence and passivity in the face of evil. Such tactics may, in the short term, preserve a semblance of what Van Dusen likes to refer to as "the public peace" and "our legal order" (518), but in so doing they conceal an underlying violence and disorder, and thus exert no moderating effect upon the overall situation; indeed, the false moderation of complacency is likely to result only in an eventual confrontation that is all the more extreme for being so long suppressed. Recognizing that complacency and hatred constitute *complementary* forms of extremism, King had the courage to pursue the course of non-violent direct action, a course that was not only more difficult but, in the true sense of the term, more moderate.

Note that Paragraph 1 has a point, but the quotations used in support of this point provide only a very limited form of illustration; they do not help to advance an argument or analysis that would elaborate or develop this point. Moreover, the quoted material is thrown in without regard to the grammatical coherence of the paragraph and in a manner that refers to unquoted material. What are these "two forces" that are included in the first sentence? Who is referred to in the phrase "his repressed emotions"? By contrast, Paragraph 2 makes proportionately much smaller use of quotations but uses them more effectively to advance the author's argument. Here the quoted material clearly plays a supporting role, one that is crucially important to the author's purpose but that does not overshadow it.

Rebound Quotations

Quotations can also provide a handy way to set up your own arguments and claims by first "bouncing off" or rebounding a quotation that argues *against* your stance. Such quotations will usually offer assertions that you intend to refute or rebut, and care should be taken with this technique in order to avoid having your entire paper become a kind of "point-counterpoint" list. Here is one example of the appropriate use of a rebound quotation:

> One may also detect a note of cynical disrespect in Van Dusen's rather weighty lament that "[t]ragically, when civil disobedients for lack of faith abstain from democratic involvement, they help attain their own gloomy prediction" that democracy has failed (508). At least in terms of the civil rights movement, this argument simply ignores history. Prior to the sit-ins, freedom rides, boycotts and other acts of civil disobedience of the 1960s, African Americans in the South had no effective access to the democratic process. Indeed, in the face of rigged voter eligibility restrictions and overt physical intimidation it is remarkable that any African Americans retained sufficient "faith" in democracy to enroll in voter registration classes, and neither this faith nor the registration movement itself could have been sustained without recourse to civil disobedience. What was tragic about this period in American history was not any "lack of faith" on the part of protestors—I doubt that their sacrifices, including in some cases the sacrifice of life itself, could have been made without the greatest degree of religious and political faith—but rather the *bad faith* of those who manipulated civic and democratic institutions in an effort to prevent others from attaining their political rights and human potential.

Incorporating Quotations: Some Strategies

Here are some strategies you can use to incorporate quotations smoothly into your essay:

Quoting Strong Claims by the Author

These forms are useful to introduce material that the quoted author asserts in a very explicit manner:

{Author}	claims argues states asserts maintains	that	{Quotation or Paraphrase}

For example:

> Brenan asserts that "Nancy Cruzan is entitled to choose to die with dignity" (644).

> Wilson claims that crack cocaine is a much more dangerous drug than heroin (567). (*paraphrase*)

> Broder maintains that, as Americans, "we are losing confidence in our future" (637).

Quoting Weaker Claims by the Author

This form is useful to refer to material that an author advances in a more tentative manner.

	suggests		
	implies		
{Author}	indicates	that	{Quotation or Paraphrase}
	hints		
	insinuates		

For example:

> Beck hints that schools lack the expertise and competence necessary to administer birth control and sex education programs (458). (*paraphrase*)

> Beck suggests that "[w]hen the schools can't even do a good job of teaching academics, it's grasping at straws to expect they can be effective in reducing AIDS and teen pregnancies" (458).

Linking Quotations to the Points They Support

It is important to link quotations to the points they are being used to support. Words and phrases that are very useful for this purpose include "thus," "for example," and "for instance."

Thus,				
For example,	{Author}	{Argues/Suggests}	that	{Quotation}.
For instance,				

For example:

Erikson believes that the decision to employ an atomic weapon against Japan was not given sufficient thought or reflection. For example, he maintains that "there were few military or logistic reasons for striking as sharply as we did and that the decision to drop moved on the crest of an almost irreversible current" (469).

Cohen takes the position that the inability of animals to make moral judgments means that they cannot be said to have rights. He argues, for instance, that "[o]nly in a community of beings capable of self-restricting moral judgments can the concept of a right be correctly invoked" (494).

Minot feels that we too often overlook economic considerations in our analysis of student performance. Thus, he suggests that "[p]erhaps the reason American education has declined so markedly is because America has raised a generation of part-time students" (274).

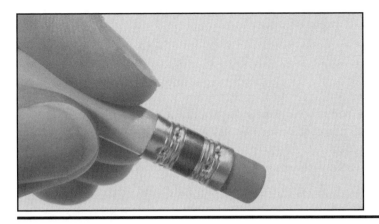

Revision

Revision plays a crucial role in almost all the writing that we do, whether in college or a career. Some even point to the credo that "all writing is re-writing," suggesting that any written expression represents the re-working of the ideas and values the writer draws upon. There is some truth to this notion, since even invention and drafting are recursive activities that involve the reworking of ideas almost at the same time that they are being initially articulated. But revision should really be understood, more significantly, as *re-vision*, a careful re-seeing and reconceptualization of one's original ideas. Revision in this sense is what allows writing to achieve a depth and insight that go beyond one's "first take" or initial understanding of an issue. Revision thus accounts for much of the epistemological power of writing: by diligently reconsidering and reworking our arguments we come to understand them more completely and express them more eloquently.

As a general rule, the most thoughtful and creative concepts and arguments in your paper will not be the ones that occur to you first, but those which arise thereafter as you revisit and refocus your words and ideas. It is therefore important in approaching any writing project to have a desire to go beyond your initial impressions, not only in terms of developing ideas during prewriting but also in terms of reconsidering them during revision. The strength of your writing will usually depend upon your ability to rework and improve what you achieve in your initial drafts. Keep in mind that few "A" papers would receive such a mark in their first-draft versions and that a writing process that does not reserve enough time for genuine revision is likely to result in weak papers.

In thinking about revision, it is useful to keep two distinctions in mind:

Corrective vs. Reflective Revision

Corrective revision refers to the kinds of changes made to fix obvious errors or to address obvious shortcomings. You will usually find yourself engaged in corrective revision even when completing your first draft, and you should always save time for thorough corrective revision (i.e., proofreading) of your final draft. In college, it is simply assumed that a writer will eliminate most grammatical or mechanical errors before a paper is submitted, and papers that disappoint this expectation are likely to be penalized.

Reflective revision is concerned not with correcting errors but rather with reflecting upon the conceptual quality of a paper and considering how its ideas might be augmented and improved. You should make sure that reflective revision is part of your writing process on any writing project. The Writing Center can be particularly helpful to you when you undertake this sort of revision.

Surface vs. Global Revision

Surface revision addresses editing at the word and sentence-level. While surface revision often involves error-correction, the term is not entirely synonymous with corrective revision, for surface revision can also address issues of style or tone that involve questions of judgment and purpose rather than simple choices of correct or incorrect grammar or usage.

Global revision pertains to revision at the level of paragraphs or multi-paragraph sections. While it is natural to engage in corrective sorts of surface revision during the drafting process, it is not a good idea to do an exhaustive job of surface revision before you have completed global changes. Since global revision may result in the elimination or radical restructuring of large sections of text, you would be wasting time if you were to polish a paragraph that later needs to be deleted.

Global Revision

Global revision entails literally re-visioning that which you have previously written. Most writers realize that after putting aside a piece of writing for a while, after gaining some critical distance from it, they can usually pick it up again and find several points that would benefit from polishing. This process usually doesn't require scrapping the entire work and starting fresh. Still, it does mean reviewing the thesis, arguments, organization, proof, and conclusions of a paper, always with an eye to making them clearer, more succinct, and more persuasive. Writing is a *practice*, a lifelong pursuit. We can continue to improve as writers for as long as we write, and our writing itself can continue to be improved through revision.

Common Problems

The "Analytical Terms" described in Part III of the *Course Book* provide a compact yet productive framework with which to analyze and comment upon the global strengths and weaknesses of a text, and one that may be used by both instructors and students. When papers are returned to you, you should take time to read the comments carefully to make sure you understand them (ask your instructor about any marks or comments that you find unclear) and to consider not simply what they suggest about your paper itself but, even more importantly, what they indicate about changes you may wish to consider in your writing process. The section that follows recommends some ways to go about this. It is important, however, to recognize that sometimes papers exhibit what might be termed imbalanced characteristics, in which the very strengths of a paper may be implicated in its weaknesses. Such cases are not uncommon and should be handled with particular care and thoughtfulness, since they usually indicate the need to break away from writing habits that may be deeply ingrained.

The five genres described here occur with some frequency:

Form without Substance

+ CONTROL — COGENCY

The most common example of this type of writing is, of course, the five-paragraph essay. When writers who produce such writing also have a knack for academic cant (i.e., + STYLE), it can be difficult to convince them (or sometimes even to recognize) that there's no "there" there. Be aware that while structure is crucial in writing, saying nothing in a well-organized fashion is still saying nothing and will not earn you high marks.

Playing It Safe

+ ADDRESSING THE ISSUE — COGENCY

Papers of this sort talk *around* the topic without ever directing themselves *toward* it. While the paper may spin a web of ideas connecting various issues in the assignment, the spider is missing: your *own* ideas aren't stated. Your analysis may be praiseworthy, but you need to be more assertive in setting forth your own position.

Only One Way

+ COGENCY — ADDRESSING THE ISSUE

These papers argue with such single-minded vehemence that the issues at stake in the topic are likely to be obscured or ignored. While your commitment to your argument should be evident, keep in mind that a convincing essay displays not just energy but insight, particularly with regard to opposing perspectives on the issues being discussed.

Details, Details

+ SUPPORT — COGENCY
— CONTROL

These papers simply accumulate details without regard to their relevance or significance. Sometimes such writing is the result of appositional or "bottom-up" thinking, a mindset inclined to work at the level of anecdote rather than that of proposition. You will need to focus on organizing facts within a framework of pertinent assertions that establish the *meaning of details*.

Quick and Dirty

+ COGENCY	— CONTROL
+ ADDRESSING THE ISSUE	— GRAMMAR AND MECHANICS
+ SUPPORT	— STYLE

An unfortunately common type, this kind of writing may be the result of time pressure, simple lassitude, or a romantic faith in unmediated inspiration. You should spend more time planning the essay and allow ample time for revision.

Addressing Six Common Problems

Problem 1: Lack of Conceptual Depth

Check Prewriting Process

Do the prewriting materials indicate that you spent enough time on invention? What inscriptive methods (clustering, listing, freewriting, etc.) did you use? (If your paper hasn't connected ideas, perhaps clustering might help; if certain arguments don't seem to have been thought through, perhaps focused freewriting would help you find what you want to say.) Have you attempted to move beyond initial impressions, as by employing heuristic prompts? Have you developed and selected ideas, or merely recorded truisms and common knowledge?

Potential responses:

> Spend more time on invention: no piece of writing is likely to surpass the thinking underlying it.

> Try different inscriptive methods, using schematic methods (clustering, brainstorming) to develop a conceptual overview of the project or freewriting to develop a feel for tone or to get started.

> Consider ideas and arguments representing *various* perspectives on the issue.

Check Revision Process

Do your rough drafts *look* rough, or suspiciously tidy? How much time did you spend on revision? What *kinds* of changes did you make between the first and last drafts: global or mainly syntactic? Do the revisions represent *corrective* or *reflective* changes?

Potential responses:

> Begin the writing process earlier, to allow more time for reflection and large-scale revision.

> Allow time for cooling off periods between drafts. It's difficult to evaluate the conceptual strength of a draft during or even immediately after its production, and you'll do a better job of both corrective and reflective revision if you can come back to your work with a fresh eye.

Problem 2: Poor Organization

Check Prewriting Process

Examine your prewriting materials for evidence of global planning. Did you exit the prewriting process having achieved some sense of overall purpose, and is this purpose apparent in the structure of your paper? Or was a mechanical (e.g., five-paragraph essay) organizational format simply imposed upon the material?

Potential responses:

> If you didn't do much planning, keep in mind that almost all forms of complex human behavior depend on careful planning. The transition from prewriting to first draft shouldn't be made without first devising a rough plan.

> If you used an outline, consider whether it was too open and indefinite, or, at the opposite extreme, too rigid and restrictive.

Check Revision Process

Check the sequence of drafts for signs of global restructuring: the addition, deletion, combination, or transposition of paragraphs or sections of paragraphs.

Potential responses:

> If there are few signs of paragraph-level revision, remember that such changes should be part of the revision process and that they usually take precedence over surface-level revision. Look for spots where paragraphs might be added, deleted, combined, shifted, or split.

> If you skipped making a plan and tried instead to organize the paper solely through drafts and freewriting, keep in mind that this is probably the most time-consuming method for structuring writing. While freewriting results in good tone and texture (and is thus a mainstay of fiction writers), it may not be the most efficient approach given the time constraints on most college writing projects. A novelist may take years to finish a book, but you may only have three weeks to complete a paper.

Problem 3: Weak Development or Support

Check Prewriting Process

Analyze your prewriting materials: Is the material primarily abstract or concrete? Did you try to develop detailed and specific support for your ideas? Were you able to connect the points you wanted to make to relevant supporting material?

Potential responses:

> Remember that it is crucial to relate fact and idea during invention. After recording a fact or detail, think of the point it might support; after jotting down an idea, try to record the concrete facts or details it brings to mind.

> During prewriting, as you select the points you may wish to make, take time to cull through all prewriting materials looking for relevant support. Points and supporting information may then be connected in the form of a rough outline or plan.

Check Revision Process

Analyze the sequence of your drafts: Do successive revisions show a deepening of supporting information?

Potential responses:

> Look for paragraphs that are insufficiently developed and consider what facts or details might be used to strengthen the paragraph's support. In doing this, it often helps to go back over your prewriting materials to see if you can find relevant but unused information.

> Look for paragraphs that contain *only* supporting information. Consider whether an appropriate cueing sentence might be added to provide the paragraph with a "point," or whether the paragraph might be combined with another containing such a point already.

> Pay attention to any "loose" supporting material that is floating around in several paragraphs and that might be more effectively consolidated within a single paragraph.

Problem 4: Weak Thesis or Wandering Argument

Potential responses:

Here you want to consider what the main purpose of your paper is and where this purpose is expressed to the reader *in the text of the essay.* To follow your argument, the reader will need a thesis and additional paragraph-level cues throughout the paper.

> If the main purpose has not been declared, remember that your reader can only read your paper, not your mind. If you yourself have difficulty recalling or defining the purpose of the paper, then you probably need to return to prewriting.

> If the main purpose is announced too far down in the paper, "raise" the thesis into the introduction. If you were intentionally trying to reserve your thesis to achieve a surprise ending or to avoid alienating a hostile audience, remember to provide at least a main direction for the paper early on—something to guide the reader's interpretation.

> If the main purpose is weakly or only implicitly expressed, consider ways to strengthen or clarify it. This usually entails revising your thesis.

> Ask yourself whether each paragraph advances the purpose or thesis of the paper and then consider how you have set up and cued the relationship between each paragraph claim and the overall thesis of the paper.

> If a paragraph does not seem to advance the paper's main argument, consider whether the paragraph is entirely off-topic or merely miscued.

Problem 5: One-Sided Argument

Potential response:

Remember that you have not only a right but also an *obligation* to argue what you genuinely believe to be true, but that to do so effectively requires that you take account of and address the values and beliefs of the discourse community in which you are writing. This is particularly important within the academic discourse community. To make your argument more balanced, consider the opposing positions carefully and modify your position accordingly. You may wish to concede points on which you agree with your opponents, and you will certainly want to rebut their most salient points.

Problem 6: Writer-Based Prose

Potential responses:

Look for passages that are perfectly comprehensible to you yet which are likely to be very difficult for the reader to understand. Because this is difficult for you to judge, it helps to read the paper aloud to yourself or (better yet) to someone else. Look for private information or a personal perspective that the average reader probably cannot share with you.

> Try to judge what kind of *world knowledge* a reader would need to understand your paper the way you wish; then consider how such information might be supplied, as through the addition of background information in your introduction.

> Consider the kind of *expectations* you want the reader to bring to the paper. Then look for ways to *cue* such expectations.

> Analyze the characteristics of the audience the paper is addressing and the assumptions you can properly make about that audience's knowledge and expectations.

Methods for Analyzing Global Qualities of Papers

Cogency

> What is the paper as a whole attempting to achieve? What is it mainly about, and what is it arguing?

> How insightful and creative is the paper? Does it show originality of thought, or does it mainly reiterate arguments that are commonly made about its topic? Does it *contribute* anything to the reader's mindset?

> How forceful is the paper's main point (main line of argument)?

Addressing the Issues

> Does the paper as a whole engage the assigned writing task? How completely and directly does it do so? Does the paper address the complexity of the issue, making effective use of counterarguments?

> Does the paper display "meta-engagement," an authorial purpose that encompasses without obscuring the purpose required by the writing task? Does the essay seem to have an organic purpose, one to please the writer, or does it merely "answer the question"?

> What is each paragraph doing to advance your point?

> How effectively is each paragraph's purpose signaled? Is this purpose *directly relevant* to your point regarding the assigned issue?

Support

> Are your points effectively supported? What paragraph-level arguments might be *added* to the paper? Look particularly for undersupported claims within paragraphs that might be developed into paragraphs of their own.

> Does the paper contain irrelevant paragraphs that need to be deleted or combined with others?

> Does supporting material need to be more closely tied to the paper's main line of argument?

Style/Grammar and Mechanics

> Is the style of the paper elegant, clean, and mature?

> Does the language of the paper provide implicit reinforcement for its argument?

> Does the tone of the paper speak well of you as an author?

Control

> How clear or apparent is the paper's main point or main line of argument, both in the introduction and throughout the paper?

> Does the paper contain "jumps" within or between paragraphs?

> Do paragraphs and sections of paragraphs serve a clear function in advancing the author's point regarding the assigned issue?

Function Outline

A function outline consists of brief statements that explain how each paragraph in your essay functions in relationship to your thesis. Creating a function outline gives you a more critical perspective on your essay and helps you identify the need for thesis and paragraph-level revisions.

Steps for Creating a Function Outline:

1. Number the paragraphs in the body of your essay (i.e., exclude paragraphs making up the introduction and conclusion).

2. Write your thesis statement at the top of your function outline.

3. Read through your essay paragraph by paragraph and note under "Function" what each paragraph is *doing* to support your thesis. Common paragraph functions include:

    > presenting background information

    > developing a main supporting argument

    > making a concession

    > rebutting a counterargument

4. Read through each paragraph again and record the topic sentence(s). If you cannot locate one in a paragraph, look for word cues that refer back to your thesis—you can use these words to develop topic sentences.

5. Once you have worked through each individual paragraph, analyze the function outline as a whole and consider the following:

    > Do the thesis and the body of the essay match?

    > Is each paragraph cued effectively?

    > Is each paragraph sufficiently developed?

    > Are there redundant paragraphs?

    > Are there missing paragraphs?

    > Does the sequence of paragraphs make logical sense?

Function Outline Form

Thesis Statement: _____

_____

_____

Paragraph 1:

  Function: _____

  Topic Sentence: _____

Paragraph 2:

  Function: _____

  Topic Sentence: _____

Paragraph 3:

  Function: _____

  Topic Sentence: _____

Paragraph 4:

  Function: _____

  Topic Sentence: _____

Paragraph 5:

  Function: _____

  Topic Sentence: _____

Paragraph 6:

  Function: _____

  Topic Sentence: _____

Paragraph 7:

  Function: _____

  Topic Sentence: _____

Surface Revision

The global-revision process necessarily touches on sentence-level expression and formatting. However, surface revision deserves close attention in itself. Your authority as an author is undermined by sloppy "technical" errors of formatting, spelling, and usage. Furthermore, attention to the grammatical and syntactical infelicities that creep into successive drafts of an essay pays off in improved readability. Note, however, that merely technically correct writing will not likely earn high marks; form needs substance.

Addressing Six Common Problems

Problem 1: Syntactic Errors

Check Revision Process

Examine the *intensity* and *timing* of your surface-level revisions. Approximately what percentage of the sentences have you modified? What kinds of changes have been made? With what apparent purpose? When have syntactic revisions been made: in early drafts, late drafts, or throughout?

Potential responses:

> If there is little evidence of syntactic revision, reserve time expressly for this purpose.

> If you tend to make obvious errors, errors that plainly do not represent your normal grammatical competence as a *speaker*, then make it a practice to read drafts *aloud*, or have someone else read the draft while you listen.

> If a pattern of error is apparent (fragments, run-ons, and comma splices being the most common), then make it a habit *late* in the writing process to dedicate a read-through solely to the task of identifying and correcting instances of the target error.

Problem 2: *General Carelessness*

Potential response:

The best way to handle careless mistakes is simply by remembering that they can make you appear much less competent than you probably would like to be considered. Careless spelling errors, for example, seldom prevent anyone from reading and understanding a paper, but they may do a great deal to lower the reader's opinion of the writer. Be sure to allow yourself enough time to proofread slowly and conscientiously.

Problem 3: *Passive Voice*

In many (but not all) contexts, English word order favors placing the doer (or agent) of an action as the subject of a sentence, ahead of the verb (which names the action) and of the object (which names what was "done-to"). Sentences that place the agent of an action in the position of the grammatical subject are called active:

Active:	While quail-hunting, Dick Cheney shot Harry Whittington.
Passive:	While quail-hunting, Harry Whittington was shot by Dick Cheney.

Sometimes a passive sentence will drop any reference to the agent who did the action. This kind of sentence is known as an agentless passive:

Agentless Passive: Harry Whittington was shot while quail-hunting.

The active form of a sentence is generally clearer, cleaner, and more direct than the passive form. Passive sentences waste words and often confuse the subject-agent relationship. Furthermore, passive voice sentences often conceal the subject's responsibility for actions.

Potential responses:

> Identify the linking verbs (*am, is, are, was, were, be, being, been*) and rewrite the sentence to eliminate them. This procedure in itself usually resolves passive-voice problems.

> Consider carefully who or what bears responsibility for the action in the sentence. The agent should act as the subject of the sentence.

> Eliminating passive construction often leads you to vary the syntax of sentences or to combine sentences, with positive stylistic benefits.

Problem 4: Diction

Check Revision Process

Is the language you use appropriate for both the topic and the discourse community? Have you made significant diction changes from draft to draft? Have you found yourself relying on the thesaurus? Are you making your argument clearly and simply, or are you substituting fancy language in an attempt to compensate for underdeveloped thought?

Potential responses:

> If you have any doubt about the correct usage of word, strike it and substitute simpler language.

> Remain alert to idiomatic expressions. Often these problems result from incorrect prepositions (e.g., the incorrect "based off of" rather than the correct "based on").

> Avoid loading sentences with polysyllabic words. As research has shown, using too many long Latinate words in a sentence actually interferes with readers' comprehension.

Problem 5: Formatting

Following the conventions of manuscript formatting and "technical" style indicates to the reader your familiarity with the conventions of the academic-discourse community. Clean formatting helps build your credibility as an author.

Potential responses:

> Your essay must have a title. You should not boldface, italicize, underline, or place in quotation marks your own title.

> Print on one side of the paper only. *All* text should be double-spaced. Do not leave extra spaces between the title and the first paragraph nor between paragraphs.

> Use 1" margins all around unless your instructor requests exact MLA format, which would mean 1", with 1.25" on the left margin.

> Do not justify (align) the right margin. Only the left margin is justified.

> Number your pages in the upper right-hand corner. You should not, however, number your *first page*. Your Works Cited page should be numbered as part of the whole paper.

> Use a standard 12-point serif font, such as Times New Roman (the font used here). Do not use sans-serif fonts such as **Arial** or Futura. Do not use "creative" fonts such as **this one**.

> As per MLA format, your bibliographic references pages should bear the title Works Cited.

> Do not use footnotes, but parenthetical citations.

Problem 6: Redundancy

Check Revision Process

What changes have you made to express your argument as clearly and succinctly as possible? Have you made an effort to eliminate "deadwood" from your sentences? As you have made global revisions, has your writing become unintentionally wordy?

Potential responses:

> Eliminate unessential adjectives and adverbs. Especially late in the writing process, you may discover that you have been using modifiers as a "crutch."

> Carefully examine modifying phrases and clauses. You may find that they simply repeat material in sentences' main clauses.

> Make a point of combining sentences into clearer, shorter units. You can assume that your reader has wits enough to follow your main line of argument without your having to detail every step.

Part II

WORKING WITH OUTSIDE SOURCES

SECTION 1: Using Source Materials

SECTION 2: Documentation Conventions

Using Source Materials

Overview

Writing projects for Writing 150 usually require you to develop a thesis or a position on an issue, and that position is often given breadth and support by the use of outside sources. Although these papers involve outside "research," they are not expected to be excessively long or to incorporate a great many sources; that is, these papers are not intended to be long, information-based research papers that attempt to cover a topic exhaustively. Instead, papers written for courses in the Writing Program have been designated as "researched" papers; that is, they are expected to be *purposeful* position papers that develop a strong argument, *utilizing*, not simply displaying, outside sources. A researched paper has the following characteristics:

1. it is a relatively short paper (5–7 pages);

2. it has the purpose of developing a position on a genuine issue;

3. it integrates material from outside sources as a means of developing and supporting its main point.

In working with outside sources, you should employ evidence drawn from various sources in a manner that does not displace or obscure the centrality of your *own* ideas and *own* writing. In particular, writing that draws upon textual material (the research*ed* paper) should exhibit a clear thesis and a strong personal voice; it should not merely string together chunks of information or opinions obtained from other sources. You should undertake research, whether from assigned readings or other sources, in order to formulate an informed position on a complex issue, not simply to exhibit research ability. Toward this end, research*ed* papers will generally incorporate no more than five or six sources.

Requirements for Writing an Acceptable Researched Paper

In writing a researched paper, you should:

1. Establish the centrality of your own ideas and your own writing style.

2. Indicate awareness of your audience and of various perspectives regarding the issue.

3. Understand the consequences and implications of your approach to the issue.

4. Develop an effective argumentative structure.

5. Use evidence effectively to support your argument or analysis.

6. Make the writing lively through anecdote and example.

7. Acknowledge and document sources correctly.

Research Basics

The Importance of Assuming an Active Role

The process of research should be engaged in actively, and to assume an active role, you should begin by exploring the topic in terms of your own experience and ideas. Use some invention strategies, jot down several possible ideas for a thesis, or even write a rough draft of the essay in order to focus your thinking. Of course, reading outside sources will cause your ideas to change as you discover more information and alternative possibilities. But thinking about your topic in advance will enable you to search for information in a more focused way and evaluate what you find with greater insight.

Active researchers reflect as they read and take notes—they do not simply record information mechanically or highlight information without thinking about why and how they might use it. Remember that the goal of examining outside sources is not simply to "learn" or memorize information, but rather to consider how new information or a particular perspective corresponds to what you already know about a topic (whether or not you find such a perspective convincing) and how it might be used in your essay. As you read, keep in mind the nature of the writing task (in fact, keep a copy with you and refer to it frequently) and consider how the information and ideas you are discovering can best help you fulfill that task.

Distinguishing between Primary and Secondary Sources

Essays written in Writing 150 may utilize both primary and secondary sources, and it is important to understand the difference between them if you decide to include a source in your essay. A **primary source** contains information taken directly from the original source and can include interviews and conversations, surveys, experiments, or questionnaires. A document containing raw data compiled by the Census Bureau, the *Declaration of Independence*, or a literary work such as a novel or a poem are examples of a primary source. A **secondary source** is any type of commentary on the primary source and is interpretive, at least to a certain extent. An article that analyzes census data, for example, may be oriented toward a particular political agenda, and an analysis of the *Declaration of Independence* may have a specific legal purpose. Because you want to understand as much as possible about the works you are quoting and the reason these works were written, it is therefore necessary to examine secondary sources carefully and to be alert for possible bias.

The Function of Outside Sources

"Tips For Using Outside Sources in a Paper" (see the following) poses questions about *why* you might wish to include information from a published work in your essay—that is, to consider what role a source might play in supporting your thesis. Do not include elements from other texts simply to fill up space. Any outside source you cite, whether in the form of direct quotation, paraphrase, or summary, should be used for some purpose—to develop and support your ideas or to set up counterarguments against which your essay will then argue.

In terms of the *number* of sources to include, be careful about letting outside material replace your own claims or propositions so that the paper consists simply of a long list of quotations. Use other texts economically, rely on brief excerpts for most purposes, and employ block quotations sparingly, if at all. The key is to use enough sources to support your position, but not so many that your own perspective is lost.

Paraphrasing Sources

Paraphrasing is a more active way of incorporating material from outside sources than is direct quotation because it requires you to rephrase someone else's statements in your own words. In order to paraphrase, you will have to think about a passage, understand its meaning, and translate that meaning into your own language. When you incorporate paraphrase into your essay, you must refer to the author of the idea you are including and provide an appropriate citation.

Summarizing Sources

Summarizing is also a more active way of incorporating material from outside sources than is direct quotation because it requires you pick out the main points of a passage, article, or book and restate these points using your own words. When you incorporate a summary into your essay, you must refer to the author of the idea you are including. Although you are not using the author's exact words, the idea came from a published work, and therefore the author must be credited and the source cited.

Acknowledging and Documenting Sources

When a writing project requires the inclusion of outside sources, it is important that these sources be *acknowledged* and *documented*. The following material focuses on incorporating material from outside sources into the body of your text and on acknowledging sources properly according to the MLA (Modern Language Association) and the APA (American Psychological Association) systems. Faculty in the Writing Program usually require the MLA system. However, it is important to keep in mind that the method of documentation varies according to academic discipline, and that when you are writing papers for courses in other departments, you should check with your instructor about which method to use. The USC Writing Center has several textbooks that outline different methods of acknowledging and documenting sources, and the college library has many different manuals on reserve, which you will be able to use. These include the following:

MLA Handbook for Writers of Research Papers

> This outlines the MLA system, which is preferred in most disciplines in the humanities, including philosophy, religion, and history.

Publication Manual of the American Psychological Association

> This outlines the APA system, which is preferred in most disciplines in the social sciences, including sociology, political science, and economics.

Chicago Manual of Style

> This manual is designed as a guide to suitable style in the presentation of term papers, theses, and dissertations in both scientific and nonscientific fields.

Please also note that styles do change and evolve over time. The limited examples presented in the following pages may be current now and sufficient for use in Writing 150, but you should always acquire the latest edition of the appropriate manual to check citation requirements when embarking on a major writing project. In addition, the increasing use of Internet resources has given rise to a whole new series of citation issues, and citation standards for electronic sources are rapidly evolving. The following online resources provide helpful (and generally up-to-date) tips for citing such sources:

Duke University's *Guide to Library Research: Citing Sources*

> https://library.duke.edu/research/citing

Purdue University's *Using MLA Format* and *Using APA Format*

> https://owl.english.purdue.edu/owl/resource/747/01/
>
> https://owl.english.purdue.edu/owl/resource/664/01/

Avoiding Plagiarism

Learning to acknowledge and document sources properly will enable you to avoid being charged with plagiarism, which not only can be embarrassing but can also prevent you from reaching educational and professional objectives. Some plagiarism is actually unintentional—students do not acknowledge their sources simply because they are unaware of the importance of doing so and are unacquainted with scholarly methods. The following material, then, will help you avoid plagiarism, either deliberate or inadvertent. Of course, proper documentation of sources is also important for helping your readers locate your references, if they are interested in doing so. It also indicates that you are a serious student who is aware of what has been written about the topic and who understands the importance of acknowledging other people's work.

When to Document Outside Sources

In writing most university papers, you will be expected to consult outside sources and incorporate the work of previous scholars into your analysis or argument. Much of this section of the *Course Book* illustrates the proper format to use when documenting sources. However, student writers must also know when to document a source. Failure to document ideas or words borrowed from others is a serious violation of academic honesty, whether or not it is intentional. Although the most blatant form of plagiarism is to repeat another writer's words more or less verbatim, other forms, often less obvious, are also considered plagiarism. Carefully study the following examples, modeled on those in the *MLA Handbook for Writers of Research Papers* (New York: MLA, 1988. 21–25.). They illustrate the most common forms of plagiarism, the differences between legitimate paraphrase and plagiarism, and acceptable ways to eliminate plagiarism.

Example 1: Repeating Another's Words without Acknowledgement

Original Source (From Neil Postman. *Amusing Ourselves to Death*. New York: Penguin, 1985. 127–128.)

> The television commercial is the most peculiar and pervasive form of communication to issue forth from the electric plug....The move away from the use of propositions in commercial advertising began at the end of the nineteenth century. But it was not until the 1950's that the television commercial made linguistic discourse obsolete as the basis for product decisions. By substituting images for claims, the pictorial commercial made emotional appeal, not tests of truth, the basis of consumer decisions.

Plagiarized Version (essentially verbatim)

> Television commercials have made language obsolete as a basis for making decisions about products. The pictorial commercial has substituted images for claims and thereby made emotional appeal, rather than tests of truth, the basis of consumer decisions.

Although the writer has changed, rearranged, and deleted words in the version above, the text is essentially the same as the original source. In paraphrasing, you take the writer's ideas and put them in your own words. It is *not* a process of substituting synonyms or rearranging the order of words. Even if the version above gave credit to Postman for his ideas, the passage would be considered plagiarized.

Correctly Paraphrased and Documented Version

> Postman argues that television commercials do not use language or "tests of truth" to help viewers decide whether to buy a product. Instead, they rely on images to create an emotional appeal that influences consumers' decisions (127–128).

In the correctly paraphrased and documented version above, *most of the ideas* have been paraphrased or restated in the writer's own words. Quotation marks have been placed around a key phrase that is taken directly from the original source. In addition, the name of the author refers readers to a corresponding entry in the Works Cited page, and the page number indicates the location of the information in the source cited.

Example 2: Presenting Another's Argument or Point of View without Acknowledgement

---

Original Source (From Arlene Skolnick. *Embattled Paradise*. New York: Basic Books, 1991: 11.)

> The changes in larger society, as well as their reverberations in the family, call into question basic assumptions about the nature of American society, its family arrangements, and Americans themselves. A "cultural struggle" ensues as people debate the meaning of change. One of these periods of cultural upheaval occurred in the early decades of the nineteenth century; a second occurred in the decades just before and after the turn of the twentieth century. For the last thirty years, we have been living through another such wave of social change.

Three related structural changes seem to have set the current cycle of family change in motion: first, the shift into a "postindustrial" information and service economy; second, a demographic revolution that not only created mass longevity but reshaped the individual and family life course, creating life stages and circumstances unknown to earlier generations; third, a process I call "psychological gentrification," which involves an introspective approach to experience, a greater sense of one's own individuality and subjectivity, a concern with self-fulfillment and self-development. This is the change misdiagnosed as narcissism.

Plagiarized Version

Three periods of cultural upheaval in the nineteenth and twentieth centuries have caused major changes in American society. The first occurred during the beginning of the nineteenth century, the second during the decades before and after 1900, and the third has been underway for the last thirty years. Three structural changes occurring during the current upheaval are primarily responsible for changes in American families. These include the development of a postindustrial information and service economy, demographics changes (including longer life spans that have created new and different life stages), and an increased sense of individuality including a desire for self-fulfillment and self-development.

The writer of the passage above correctly paraphrases Skolnick's ideas but does not give her credit for her ideas or line of argument. The version below eliminates the plagiarism by attributing the ideas to Skolnick.

Correctly Documented Version

According to Skolnick, three periods of cultural upheaval in the nineteenth and twentieth centuries have caused major changes in American society. The first occurred during the beginning of the nineteenth century, the second during the decades before and after 1900, and the third has been underway for the last thirty years. Three structural changes occurring during the current upheaval are primarily responsible for changes in American families. These include the development of a postindustrial information and service economy, demographics changes (including longer life spans that have created new and different life stages), and an increased sense of individuality including a desire for self-fulfillment and self-development (11).

In the version above, a reader would be able to locate the source by finding the title of Skolnick's book in the Works Cited page and looking on page 11, the number indicated at the end of the paragraph.

Example 3. Repeating Another Writer's Particularly Apt Phrase or Term without Acknowledgment

---

Original Source (From Arlene Skolnick. *Embattled Paradise*. New York: Basic Books, 1991: 11.)

Three related structural changes seem to have set the current cycle of family change in motion: first, the shift into a "postindustrial" information and service economy; second, a demographic revolution that not only created mass longevity but reshaped the individual and family life course, creating life stages and circumstances unknown to earlier generations; third, a process I call "psychological gentrification," which involves an introspective approach to experience, a greater sense of one's own individuality and subjectivity, a concern with self-fulfillment and self-development. This is the change misdiagnosed as narcissism.

Plagiarized Version

The large number of "self-help" books published each year attest to Americans' concern with self-improvement and achieving more fulfilling lives. This process might be described as "psychological gentrification."

Correctly Documented Version

The large number of self-help books published each year attest to Americans' concern with self-improvement and their desire to have a more fulfilling life. Skolnick labels this process as "psychological gentrification" (11).

As the previous example illustrates, putting quotation marks around a borrowed word or phrase is not sufficient documentation. You must also acknowledge the author and give the page numbers so a reader would be able to consult the original source and locate the word or phrase. In the original source, Skolnick takes credit ("a process I call") for coining the term "psychological gentrification." Quotation marks in the original appear to be used for emphasis. Phrases in quotations should be cited unless they have become common usage (e.g., "postindustrial" in the original source above).

Tips for Using Outside Sources in a Paper

The following questions will help you gain a critical perspective on published material—books, articles, and information from the Internet. Consider these questions before including material from a published work in your papers.

1. **Decide on the reliability of the source by considering the following:**

   > *The Title*

   Does the title suggest a special perspective on the topic?

   Does the title present the author's opinion on the topic?

   > *Publication Information*

   Is the publishing company well known? (for a book)

   Is the periodical (magazine, journal, newspaper) published nationally? Regionally?

   Is the periodical well respected? Does it specialize in certain subjects?

   > *Currency*

   What is the publication date of the source?

   Does the subject require current information?

   Have innovations or new information changed the way people think about the topic?

   > *Reliability*

   Does the source acknowledge other views?

   Does the source offer sufficient evidence?

   Does the source provide a historical or critical context for a discussion of the topic?

   Are adequate definitions provided?

2. **Decide why you are using a source.**

Does it support your position by providing needed authority?

Is it an example?

Does it provide important facts or statistics?

Does it represent an opposing viewpoint?

Does it provide a definition?

3. **Determine if the information is common knowledge.**

Some information may be considered "common knowledge," which means that everyone already knows it. If you include common knowledge in an essay, you do not have to document the source of your information. For example, the fact that Thomas Jefferson was the third president of the United States is considered common knowledge. But an opinion about Jefferson expressed by a social historian must be acknowledged through a citation.

4. **Incorporate sources correctly.**

Check the appropriate style sheet as specified by your teacher. Some courses will require you to use the system developed by the MLA (Modern Language Association); others will use the system developed by the APA (American Psychological Association). The system you use will determine the citation conventions both within and at the end of your paper.

Below are some general principles of incorporating quoted material into a text.

❭ The apparatus for using quotations consists of two parts:

a. By inserting quotation marks, you indicate that you are borrowing certain words as well as certain ideas that appear in your writing.

b. By inserting a citation containing the source's name, you give credit for both ideas and words to the author.

❭ There are two kinds of direct quotation:

a. *separated,* where you are distinguishing between your ideas and those of your source, and

b. *integrated,* where you are integrating your ideas with those of your source.

The simplest way to quote is to combine the citation (written by you) with the words you are quoting (exactly as they were said or written by your source). This method of quotation joins together two separate statements, with punctuation—comma or colon bridging the gap and a capital letter beginning the quoted phrase.

Chief Executive Bradley Smith stated, "The internal mechanism needs additional work."

In an alternative kind of direct quote, only the quotation marks indicate that you are using someone else's words. There is no comma or colon and no capital letter.

Chief Executive Bradley Smith stated that "the internal mechanism needs additional work."

> Extended quotation:

A quotation that runs more than four typewritten lines is set off by indenting ten spaces (or one inch) and is typed double spaced. A colon introduces the extended quotation and the quotation marks are omitted.

> Punctuating direct quotations:

a. All periods and commas are placed inside the terminal quotation marks.

b. All semicolons, colons, and dashes are placed outside the terminal quotation marks.

c. Question marks and exclamation points are sometimes placed inside the quotation marks and sometimes placed outside depending on whether they are included in the quotation.

d. Interrupting quotations by placing the citation in the middle requires four sets of quotation marks and commas on either side of the quotation.

> "I do not mind lying," wrote Butler, "but I hate inaccuracy."

e. Quoting within a quotation requires the use of both single and double quotation marks. The single quotes are used for the words quoted by your source and the double quotes are used around the words you are quoting.

> At the beginning World War I, Winston Churchill observed that "the maxim of the British people is 'Business as usual.'"

5. **Blend sources smoothly into your text to avoid the "crouton effect."**

Students sometimes throw a piece of quoted material into an essay without smoothly introducing it or commenting on it. The quotation is simply sprinkled in, without being blended into the writer's own words. As a result, the reader will crunch on the quotation, like a crouton in a salad.

a. Here is an example of the "crouton effect."

> Love is an important theme in Shakespeare's sonnets. "Let me not to the marriage of true minds/Admit impediments" (1–2).

b. Here is a version that blends the quotation into the student's text:

> The steadfastness of love is an important theme in Shakespeare's sonnets. Sonnet CXVI, which begins with the famous line, "Let me not to the marriage of true minds/Admit impediments," analyzes the nature of love and concludes that love is not really love if it "alters when it alteration finds." Love, in Shakespeare's sonnets, is something that does not change, "an ever-fixed mark./That looks on tempests and is never shaken" (1–4).

Note that the quotation is preceded by the introductory statement and followed by further elaboration. It is not simply thrown in and left to stand on its own.

6. **Use quotations sparingly.**

They generally belong in the body of your paragraph, not at the very beginning as a replacement for the topic sentence.

7. The words you use to introduce a quotation **should suggest the relationship between your own ideas** (in the previous sentence) **and the statement that you are about to quote.** You should examine the quotation before using it in order to define the way in which the author makes a point.

> Is the point being made forcefully? Use *argues, declares,* or *insists.*

> Is the statement being offered as a possibility? Use *suggests, proposes,* or *finds.*

> Does the statement immediately follow a precious reference? Use *continues* or *adds.*

Electronic Library Resources and Research Strategies

The USC Libraries provide access to hundreds of academic research databases. Most of these are licensed to USC and are not available on the free, public Internet. Use these library resources to identify articles from scholarly journals, magazines, and newspapers; to find books; and to locate other kinds of information needed for your research. Start at the Library's Home Page in the Quick Search tool bar: <http://www.usc.edu/libraries/>.

1. **Develop a Search Strategy for Your Research Topic.** What questions do you need to answer about the topic? Brainstorm for the keywords and key phrases that express the major concepts of your topic, including synonyms and related terms, concepts, or issues. Need help? Librarians at Leavey & Doheny Library can help with this and any other aspects of the research process.

2. **Find Articles: Search Multi-Subject Article Index Databases.** These article databases are good places to start. Access these from the Quick Search Databases menu at the URL above.

> **Proquest Research Library:** A multidisciplinary full-text database of scholarly, popular, and newspaper articles.

> **OmniFile Full Text Mega (H.W. Wilson):** Full text articles from thousands of scholarly journals.

> **LexisNexis:** Full text from domestic and international newspapers, news magazines and more.

> **Google Scholar:** Search scholarly literature, book chapters, articles, and more across the web. Set your institutional preferences for USC to reflect items we own.

3. **Find More Articles: Search Specialized Subject Article Index Databases.** More article indexes for specific subject areas may be accessed from a list of subjects from the databases link at "Resources by Subject" link on the home page.

4. **Searching an Article Indexing Database.** Use combinations of keywords that represent the key concepts of your topic. Remember to join your key words together with *and.* It is often necessary to do several different searches to find a few good articles!

5. **Evaluate Search Results.**

> Skim the list of article citations: Do your keywords appear in any of them? If so, in what context?

> Read article abstracts: How well does each article seem to pertain to your topic?

❯ What kind of information does each citation/abstract/article appear to provide about your topic? Is it a research findings report, critical analysis, editorial or commentary, news report, or investigative report?

❯ Scholarly vs. popular: what kind of article is it? Use the table below to determine its characteristics.

SCHOLARLY JOURNAL ARTICLES	POPULAR MAGAZINE ARTICLES
Published in an academic journal; may be described as "refereed" or "peer-reviewed"	Published in a popular, general interest, or news magazine
Author is expert on topic or scholar	Author may be lay reporter
Specialized audience of peers or students	Audience includes general public
Goal is to inform or present research	Goal is often to entertain or persuade
Research-based	Report events or findings of others
Includes sources: footnotes and bibliography	Sources may not be cited formally
Vocabulary is complex and technical	Vocabulary is familiar, nontechnical
Graphics used to illustrate a point	Graphics used for visual impact
Titles often include the words Journal, Review, or Annals (e.g., *Anthropology & Education Quarterly, Journal of Higher Education*)	Titles are often general, usually catchier (e.g., *People Weekly, Newsweek*)
Published monthly, quarterly, semi-annually, or annually	Published weekly or monthly

6. **Locate Articles.** Most article index databases contain a proportion of articles in full text; however, some do not. If the database contains only citations and abstracts, you can request the complete article for free using Interlibrary Loan services through the Find-It @ USC button found in the databases.

7. **Search for Books at USC.** *Quick Search*, on the USC Library's website, lists all books and ebooks owned by the libraries on the University Park Campus. Access *the catalog* through *Quick Search* by clicking on the Books tab of the toolbar. Search for books on your topic by using broad and similar keywords that you used to search in an article index database. You may also search for specific titles and authors using the advanced search options.

Using the World Wide Web for Research

The World Wide Web, or public Internet, and its search engines (such as Google and Yahoo!) are resources with enormous potential, provided one takes an active approach to sifting through millions of web sites. Much like television, the web is a worthy subject of critique; as a source of reliable information and intelligent opinion, it has its limitations.

Part of the web's uniqueness is its anarchy: no one is in charge. This is good news for freedom of expression, but it underscores the need for selectivity on the part of the researcher. Library-based, licensed databases provide access to resources such as scholarly journals that are published and copyrighted by conventional means, ensuring a level of editorial reliability and critical review. In contrast, web sites found through search engines like Google do not undergo any kind of editorial review to judge the accuracy or reliability of their content.

Do Active Web Research: To begin searching the web actively rather than passively, you need to assume the role of referee. The validity claims (see Section 1) are one useful method for critiquing web resources.

1. **Intelligibility/Comprehensibility:** Does the resource employ a verbal and visual style that is clear, appropriate, and persuasive? Are the language and content sufficiently sophisticated, or do grammatical and typographical errors cast doubt upon the intelligibility and intelligence of the information?

2. **Validity:** Are the opinions expressed on the site supported with evidence that seems accurate, fair, and reasonable? Are the claims themselves legitimate, or does the site's purpose seem more to inflame than inform?

3. **Truthfulness or Sincerity:** Consider again the connection between authorship and authority: whose web site is this? If the site allows you to return to a preliminary home page, what does that page tell you about the motives of the site's creator? For instance, what potential bias might you anticipate regarding the issue of global warming as presented on the web site of a radical environment group? Or a web site created by a lobbying group for the coal industry? Does the site reference other resources, or does it stand alone as an uninformed, polemical opinion?

4. **Appropriateness:** What motives and values seem to underlie the purpose of the site: to persuade, inform, and analyze, or rather to entertain, outrage, promote, or sell something? Look at the site's domain name for clues to its origin: *.com* is assigned to commercial ventures; *.edu* is for colleges, universities, other educational institutions; *.org* is for nonprofit groups and organizations; and *.gov* is for U.S. government-sponsored offices and agencies.

A web source should do what a well-written Writing 150 paper should do: support its claims with evidence, document its sources, acknowledge its own biases, and give fair treatment to opposing positions.

Section 2

Documentation Conventions

Source documentation is a service to your reader and to the larger academic community. Using proper documentation style is not just about avoiding plagiarism, though that is of course an important reason for proper citation. Properly formatted source citation is the method by which academic conversations can be traced and can build on one another. During the course of your own research, you may mine the documentation of an academic article to find additional sources to consult. In turn readers may wish to use your documentation to further their own research process. In order to facilitate this exchange of information a standardized documentation format is necessary.

To document means to provide information about the sources you used in your paper. The phrase "documentation conventions" refers to the methods writers use to convey the information about those sources.

A documentation system typically consists of two parts:

1. references within the body of text, and

2. a list at the end of the paper providing bibliographic information about works consulted and cited.

All academic papers using outside sources include both parts. However, the specific style of documentation can vary according to discipline, since disciplines have become specialized and therefore place emphasis on different types of knowledge. For example, in the Works Cited section, the MLA system places the date of publication later in the citation, since knowledge in the humanities does not become dated as quickly as it might in the natural or social sciences. A 1920 edition of a Shakespeare play, for example, might be just as valid as a 1965 edition. However, in the social sciences, which use the APA system, more recent findings might contradict older findings; therefore, in that system, the date is given toward the beginning of the citation.

Differences in documentation styles are also based on what is deemed convenient or efficient. Therefore, in its "References" list, the APA style does not use quotation marks around the title of an article, nor does it capitalize major words in the title.

Some variations, though, are due simply to the conventions of different academic disciplines. When you begin writing for a particular discipline, you will be expected to demonstrate that you are familiar with its documentation practices. The information below provides some basic information about acknowledging and documenting sources according to the MLA and APA formats. You should also keep in mind the following tips:

1. **Be scrupulous** about acknowledging secondary source material. Do not risk plagiarizing whether deliberately or inadvertently.

2. **Form is important.** Always check to see that you have the proper form for referring to outside material within the body of your text and for listing on the Works Cited or References page. Remember that proper form includes specifics such as indentation and punctuation. If you are writing for a course within a specific discipline, look over journals for that discipline. Note the system of documentation within those journals. Understanding the form requires concentration, so leave sufficient time for documenting your sources correctly.

3. **Keep a set of rules handy** when you polish your final draft. It is almost impossible to memorize every specific rule about documenting sources. The rules in this guidebook will help you use the correct forms for most papers in lower division courses. For more complete information, consult the *MLA Handbook* or the *APA Publication Manual*. These can be purchased at the USC Pertusati Bookstore or checked out from the Leavey Library.

The MLA System

In 2016, the Modern Language Association (MLA) published an 8th edition of its MLA Handbook. In keeping with its name, the MLA aims in this new edition to connect its documentation conventions with modern academic writers' needs. The 8th edition recognizes that, for 21st-century researchers, the scope of sources available in the digital age makes it impractical to maintain unique formats for each type of source included in the bibliographic information at the end of the paper. Therefore, the MLA Handbook has revised much of its documentation conventions in order to simplify and even standardize citations across different resources. In essence: instead of suggesting different rules for each source (traditional book, online book, Facebook, Twitter, etc.), the 8th edition provides a user-friendly format based on the traits shared by most works. This shift allows the writer a bit more autonomy when it comes to abiding by documentation conventions, but that also means the writer has an equally weighted responsibility to be consistent and aware of audience. With these broad concepts about the MLA revisions in mind, remember that the basics have not changed: reference your sources within the body of the paper and match those to a bibliographic list of sources at the end of the paper.

Parenthetical Reference and a Works Cited Page

According to the MLA system, information in your paper must be acknowledged by **parenthetical reference** within the body of the paper and through a **Works Cited** page at the end. The parenthetical reference provides your reader with enough information to locate the full reference in the Works Cited section, and the Works Cited page provides enough information for the reader to obtain exactly the source you used. Remember that any information or point of view which you obtained from an outside source must be acknowledged, whether it is a quotation, a summary or a paraphrase. It is better to be painstakingly meticulous about acknowledging your sources than to plagiarize unintentionally.

Parenthetical Documentation in the MLA System

In the MLA system, you should refer to outside sources within the body of your text by including enough information so that the reader will be able to locate a source in the Works Cited page at the end of the paper. Each reference to a source must provide the author's name (or a short title if the work is anonymous) and the exact page number. Here is an example:

> In diagnosing the scope of this problem, what is often overlooked is that "young men these days are as concerned about their weight as young women" (Snodgrass 237).

Note that there is no comma between the name (Snodgrass) and the page number.

Next, consider an example in which Snodgrass's name is mentioned in the accompanying text; therefore, it would not be necessary to include his name as well as the page number within parentheses:

> Snodgrass points out that "young men these days are as concerned about their weight as young women" (237).

Here, you would not need to include Snodgrass's name in the parentheses because the reader is already aware of the author's name and would be able to find the rest of the information about the source in the Works Cited section. Note also the placement of the quotation marks, the parentheses, and the period. These are conventions, which must be observed correctly.

Now suppose that your Works Cited section included two works by Snodgrass. In this case, in order for the reader to locate the source within the Works Cited section, you would have to include the title as well as the author and page number within the parentheses. Here is an illustration:

> In diagnosing the scope of this problem, what is often overlooked is that "young men these days are as concerned about their weight as young women" (Snodgrass, *Men and Appearance* 237).

The use of parenthetical documentation has made it much easier for writers to refer to outside materials. Not too long ago, students who were writing even relatively short papers had to use an elaborate system of footnotes when they included information from a secondary source.

Long Quotations

Use block quotations, indented half an inch from the margin and double-spaced, when a quotation runs more than four lines on your typewritten page. The parenthetical reference should appear two spaces after the punctuation at the end of the block. Here is an example:

> The following charming description of a day in Prague refutes the common stereotype of the bleakness of Eastern Europe:

>> The crowd of shoppers, strollers, and office workers was standing around together listening—as best I could figure out—to a comedian who must have been performing in an auditorium inside. I don't understand Czech but I guessed that it was a comedian—and a very funny one—because the staccato rhythm of his monologue, the starts, stops, and shifts of tone, seemed consciously designed to move the crowd into spasms of laughter that ripened into a rich roar. (Roth 106)

The MLA Works Cited Page

The MLA Works cited page is the place, at the end of the paper, for the more thorough bibliographic information about the sources you referenced in the body of the paper.

Here is some basic information about the Works Cited page:

1. All items are arranged in alphabetical order by the last name of the author. If no author is listed, use the first significant word of the title.

2. Each citation should begin at the left margin and additional lines in each citation should be indented five spaces (or one-half inch).

3. *Double-space* between each line and *double-space* between each citation. The title "Works Cited" should be centered one inch down from the top of the page. Then double-space between the title and the first citation.

As noted above, MLA recently shifted away from suggesting specific and different formatting conventions for each type of source. Instead, the MLA 8th Edition offers a user-friendly format comprised of simple traits of "Core Elements":

Author.

Title of Source.

Title of Container.

Other Contributors,

Version,

Number,

Publisher,

Publication Date,

Location.

Note the use of periods or commas after each Core Element. These should be part of the formatting used in your Works Cited.

Author

MLA formatting uses the term "author" loosely to denote the person or group responsible for producing the source or part of the source you have cited. Using the list above, pattern your formatting based on the Core Elements—giving attention to the periods and commas.

Title

Title should be cited in full exactly as they are identified in the source. Italicize sources that are self-contained (more on containers below) and place quotation marks around the title of a source that is part of a larger whole.

Container

The biggest change from previous MLA source documentation conventions is that MLA 8th Edition introduces **containers** as a new concept. When the source documentation is part of the larger whole, this larger whole—a periodical, website, or an edited collection for example—can be thought of as the **container**.

When the cited source is part of a larger whole, the larger whole should be considered the **container** that holds the source. For example, the container may be a collection of essays, a periodical made up of articles, a television series made up of episodes, or a Web site made up of articles, postings, or images.

A source can, however, have more than one container. It may be nested within another, larger container. A collection of poetry may be read on a digital platform such as Kindle. A journal article may be stored on a digital platform such as *JSTOR*. As more research moves online and into databases, documenting source's containers is an integral part of the research trail. A source in one container may differ from other copies, so you should represent your sources cited as accurately as possible.

Other Contributors

Other people may be credited as contributors to your sources. Editors, directors, translators, or narrators for example maybe featured in your citation. Precede each name with a description of the role:

> Adapted by
>
> Edited by
>
> Illustrated by
>
> Translated by

Version

If your source indicates that it is a version or edition of a work previously released in more than one form, identify the version/edition you used.

Number

Your source may be part of a numbered sequence. If you consult one volume out of a numbered set, denote the volume number with a prefix (Vol.). Journal issues typically contain volume and issue numbers that should be documented in your citation. For example, volume 34, issue 3 should be cited as vol. 34, no. 3.

Publisher

Identify the date your source was published. If there is more than one date, cite the date that is most meaningful or relevant to the way you've used the source. For example, a newspaper article published online may also cite the date the article appeared in print. If you only consulted the online version, note only that date and ignore the print date.

Location

The location of a source depends upon the type of source. In a print source, a page number (preceded by p.) or a page range (preceded by pp.) identifies your sources' location. The location of an online source is typically identified as its URL or Web address. There is no need to precede the Web address with http:// or www.

URLs, however, are not stable; Web publishers can change their Web address anytime. If your source offers stable URLs, called permalinks, use them in your Works Cited. Also, some online publishers assign DOIs (digital object identifiers) to their publications. These identifiers remain stable–attached to a source even if the URL changes. When possible, citing the DOI is preferable to citing a URL.

Examples:

Article Found on ProQuest Cited with DOI

Langhamer, Claire. "Love and Courtship in Mid-Twentieth Century England." *Historical Journal*,
vol. 50, no. 1, 2007, pp. 173–96. *ProQuest*, doi:10.1017/S0018246X06005966. Accessed 27 May 2009.

Online Article Cited with URL:

Lundman, Susan. "How to Make Vegetarian Chili," *eHow*,
www.ehow.com/how_10727_make-vegetarian-chili.html. Accessed 6 July 2015.

In general, here is the format citations should follow:

Author. Title. Title of container, Other contributors, Version, Number, Publisher, Publication Date, Location.

Here are some examples of these Core Elements in practice, as well as explanations for how these models conform to the MLA 8th Edition.

Citing Books
Book with One Author

Snodgrass, Stanley. *Men and Appearance*. Vanity P, 1985.

Note that the capital "P" after "Vanity" is for "Press," which when part of a longer publication name such as "Vanity Press" or "Washington Square Press" does not need to be written out or hold its own punctuation.

A Book with Two Authors

When the source has two authors, write them in the same order the source presents them. Use the "Last, First" convention for the first author and the "First Last" convention for the second author.

Johnson, Zachary, and Sandra Stone. *Living With Lunatics*. Bayberry Scott, 1975.

A Book with Three or More Authors

When a source has more than two authors, cite the first author's name using the "Last, First" convention and complete the author section with *et al.* ("and others").

Fieldstone, Jerome, et al. *Conservatism on the Rise*. Hillman, 1987.

Two or More Books by the Same Author

If you are citing two or more books by the same author, do not repeat the author's name with each entry. Instead, insert a three-hyphen line flush with the left margin. Then type a period. Below is an example:

Snodgrass, Stanley. *Men and Appearance*. Vanity P, 1985.

---. *Women and Appearance*. Vanity P, 1986.

A Book with a Translator or Editor

Lagercrantz, Olof. *From Hell to Paradise: The Comedy of Dante*. Translated by Alan Blair. Washington
Square P, 1966.

A Chapter That Is Part of an Anthology or Collection

Updike, John. "A&P." *Fiction 100*, edited by James E. Pickering, 4th ed., Macmillan, 1982, 1086–1089.

An Introduction, Preface, Foreword, or Afterward

Flintstone, Fred. Introduction. *Life in Bedrock*, by Wilma Flintstone, Stone Age P, 1982. i–ix.

Note here the use of the word "by" to distinguish the author from the writer of the introduction.

Citing Periodicals

When listing references to periodicals on the Works Cited page, you should include the same Core Elements noted above. Periodicals, because they are contained in larger works, will use the container Core Element.

Journals

For journal entries, include the title in italics, the volume number, the issue number when available, the year and inclusive page numbers:

Thomas, Jason. "How Can We Reduce the Federal Deficit?" *Journal of Economics*, vol. 12, 1992, pp. 22–24.

Magazine

Barker, James R. "Living with a Pit Bull and Loving It." *The Canine Courier*, Apr. 1989, pp. 26–29.

If the magazine comes out more frequently, add the day of the month:

von Hoffman, Nicholas. "The White House News Hole." *The New Republic*, 6 Sept. 1982, pp. 19–23.

Note that if the magazine does not indicate the name of the author, simply begin with the title of the article:

"Chaos in Television." *Time*, 12 Mar. 1979, pp. 60–61.

Newspapers

For newspaper entries, provide the author's name, the title of the article, the name of the newspaper as it appears on the front page (*Daily News*, not *The Daily News*) and the complete date (day, month, and year). Page numbers should be listed according to how they actually appear on the page. If the article does not continue on the next page, that is, if it is not printed consecutively, write only the first page number and add a + sign. Thus, if the article begins on page 15 and continues on page 36, you should write 15+.

Here is an example of a newspaper citation:

James, Noah. "The Comedian Everyone Loves to Hate." *The New York Times*, 22 Jan. 1984, p. 23.

The MLA Works Cited Page: Other Types of Sources

Some sources are neither books nor periodicals. Here are some other possibilities:

Song Titles, Films, Television or Radio Programs, Lectures, Computer Software, etc.

When referring to titles of songs, films, television or radio programs, or lectures within the text of your paper, use quotation marks for the titles of songs, lectures, or individual episodes of a television program. Italicize the titles of films and television or radio programs.

Song on a Digital Music Platform

Beastie Boys. "No Sleep Till Brooklyn." *Licensed to Ill*. Def Jam/RAL, 15 Nov. 1986, *Spotify*, open.spotify.com/album/5izHWBylmEjk1yTVPAYJWj.

Song via Online Album

Beyoncé. "Sandcastles." *Lemonade*, Parkwood Entertainment, 2016, http://www.beyonce.com/album/lemonade-visual-album/.

Song CD

Armstrong, Louis. "What a Wonderful World." *All Time Greatest Hits*. MCA. 1994.

Note: In a Works Cited entry for a song or recording that is commercially available, the person cited first (e.g., the composer or performer) will depend on the desired emphasis. Compare the two versions below:

Gershwin, George. "Foggy Day." With Wynton Marsalis, Trumpet. *Marsalis Standard Time Vol. 1*. Columbia, CK 40461, 1987.

Marsalis, Wynton, Trumpet. "Foggy Day." By George Gershwin. *Marsalis Standard Time Vol. 1*. Columbia, CK 40461, 1987.

A Published or Broadcast Interview

Shaw, Robert. *Interviews with Robert Shaw*. Interview by John Schaffer, Brentwood P, 1989.

Schwarzkopf, Norman. Interview. *Morning Edition*. National Public Radio. KCRW, 4 Jan. 1991.

Personal Interview

Smith, James. Personal Interview. 6 Nov. 1988.

The MLA Works Cited Page: The Internet

Because content published on the World Wide Web varies so widely in nature, the MLA 8th Edition citation format still suggests following the Core Elements, with special attention to the URL and (where possible) DOI information.

Below are sample citations for different kinds of sources found on the Web:

Article in an Online Academic or Professional Journal

Petitti, Diana B. "Some Surprises, Some Answers, and More Questions About Hormone Therapy." *Journal of the American Medical Association*, 294:2, 13 July 2005, pp. 245–246, doi: doi:10.1001/jama.294.2.245. Accessed 22 Mar. 2017.

Scholarly Paper

Wallace, Heather E. "Woman's Education According to Rousseau and Wollstonecraft." *Feminism and Women's Studies*, 20 Jan. 2005.

Report

Hickson, Allister. "Analytical Review: Manitoba Public Insurance Corporation Motorcycle Risk Study." University of Manitoba Transport Institute. June 2005. https://umanitoba.ca/faculties/management/ti/media/docs/Analytical_review_final_all_edits1.pdf. Accessed 7 July 2005.

Article in an Online Encyclopedia, Dictionary, or Other Reference

"Baaba Maal." *African Music Encyclopedia*. 1998, http://africanmusic.org/artists/maal.html. Accessed 7 March 2005.

Article in an Online Magazine

Epstein, Jay. "Romancing the Hedge Funds: Hollywood's New Golden Goose." *Slate*, 11 July 2005, http://www.slate.com/articles/arts/the_hollywood_economist/2005/07/romancing_the_hedge_funds.html. Accessed 22 August 2005.

Article in an Online Newspaper

Guan, Xiaofeng. "Panda Leaves Wild for Wander in City Centre." *China Daily* 18 July 2005, http://www.chinadaily.com.cn/english/doc/2005-07/18/content_461005.htm. Accessed 1 August 2005.

Professional Site

"Treating Type 2 Diabetes with Dietary Supplements. What the Science Says." National Center for Complementary and Alternative Medicine, Nov. 2013. https://nccih.nih.gov/health/providers/digest/diabetes-science.htm.

Sample MLA Works Cited Page

Here is an example of a Works Cited page. The left, right, top, and bottom margins should all be 1 inch in the MLA format, with indented text ½ inch from the left margin. All text is double-spaced.

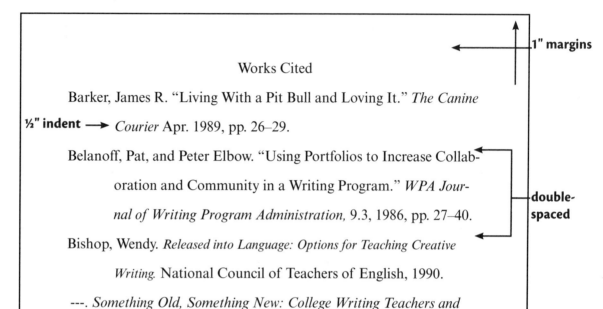

Works Cited

Barker, James R. "Living With a Pit Bull and Loving It." *The Canine*

½" indent → *Courier* Apr. 1989, pp. 26–29.

Belanoff, Pat, and Peter Elbow. "Using Portfolios to Increase Collab-

oration and Community in a Writing Program." *WPA Jour-*

nal of Writing Program Administration, 9.3, 1986, pp. 27–40.

Bishop, Wendy. *Released into Language: Options for Teaching Creative*

Writing. National Council of Teachers of English, 1990.

---. *Something Old, Something New: College Writing Teachers and*

Classroom Change. Southern Illinois UP, 1990.

"Chaos in Television." *Time.* 12 Mar. 1979, pp. 60–61.

Gardner, Howard. *Frames of Mind: The Theory of Multiple Intelli-*

gences. Basic, 1983.

Itzkoff, Dave. "Steve Martin Teaching You (and Himself) How to

Be a Comedian." *The New York Times.* 18 Apr. 2017, *https://*

www.nytimes.com/2017/04/18/arts/steve-martin-comedy-dave-

chapelle.html. Accessed 26 May 2017.

Kirschenbaum, Howard, Simon Sidney, and Rodney Napier.

Wad-Ja-Get? The Grading Game in American Education.

Hart Publishing, 1971.

Seaforth, Patricia. "The Role of Television in Presidential Elections."

Journal of American Politics 6.4, 1983, pp. 19–23.

1" margins

double-spaced

The APA System

Parenthetical Citation

In the APA system, you should refer to outside sources within the body of your text by including enough information so that the reader will be able to locate a source in the References page at the end of the paper. When using the APA system, you should write the year of publication in parentheses immediately following the author's name. If you do not mention the author by name in the text, then you should include the author's name (or a short title if the author's name is missing) and the year of publication, separated by a comma enclosed in parentheses. If you quote from your source, you must also add the page number in your parentheses, with "p" preceding the page number. Here are some examples:

> Snodgrass (1988) points out that "young men these days are as concerned about their weight as young women" (p. 237).

Note that, as in the MLA system, you would not need to include Snodgrass's name in the parentheses because it already appears in the text; that is, the reader is already aware of the author's name and would be able to find the rest of the information about the source in the References section. Note also the placement of the quotation marks, the parentheses, and the period.

In the following example, however, Snodgrass's name is not mentioned; therefore, it would be necessary to include his name as well as the page number within the parentheses:

> In diagnosing the scope of this problem, what is often overlooked is that "young men these days are as concerned about their weight as young women" (Snodgrass, 1988, p. 237).

Note the use of commas in the parentheses.

A Work with Two or More Authors

If a work has two authors, refer to both. If the names are placed within a parenthetical citation, join them with an ampersand (&).

> In a recent study of obese corporate executives (James & Jones, 1989), it was stated...

When the authors' names are used within the text, they should be joined by "and":

> James and Jones (1989) state that...

If a work has several authors (fewer than six), they should all be mentioned in the first reference:

> James, Jones, Smith, Jeeves, and Raskovsky (1987) argue...

However, in subsequent references, you can use "et al." as in:

> James et al. (1987) argue that...

The APA References Page: Books

Like the Works Cited Page in MLA form, there are also three main components in a References page: the title, the author, and the publication information (city, publisher, publication date). Here are some points to remember about the References page in the APA system:

1. All items are arranged in alphabetical order by the last name of the author. If no author is listed, use the first significant word of the title.

2. Each citation should begin at the left margin and additional lines in each citation should be indented one-half inch.

3. *Double space* between each line and *double space between each citation.* Two spaces follow a period; one space follows a comma, semicolon, or colon.

4. The title, "References," should be centered one and one-half inches down from the top of the page. Then double space between the title and the first citation.

Here are some elements of the APA style that differ significantly from the MLA style:

1. Initials, instead of full first names, are used for authors.

2. Titles of books and articles do not use capital letters, except for the first word, the first word following a colon or period within the title, and some proper nouns (e.g., names of people, places, and languages).

3. Titles of articles do not use quotation marks; other titles are italicized (not underlined).

4. There is greater emphasis on the year of publication.

Here are some examples you can use as models:

A Book with One Author

Snodgrass, S. (1985). *Men and appearance.* Los Angeles: Vanity Press.

Note that the author's first name is indicated only by an initial, that the date appears in parentheses, and that only the first word of the title begins with a capital letter.

Two or More Books by the Same Author

List two or more books by the same author in chronological order.

Snodgrass, S. (1985). *Men and appearance.* Los Angeles: Vanity Press.

Snodgrass, S. (1986). *Women and appearance.* Los Angeles: Vanity Press.

If you cite two or more works by the same author with the same year of publication, alphabetize them by title, and use lowercase letters immediately following the year to differentiate them: (1985a), (1985b), etc.

A Book with Two Authors

Reverse last name and initial for both authors, and separate them with commas. Use an ampersand (&) before the last author.

Johnson, Z., & Stone, S. (1975). *Living with lunatics.* New York: Bayberry Scott.

A Book with a Translator or Editor

Lagercrantz, O. (1966). *From hell to paradise: The comedy of Dante.* (Alan Blair, Trans.). New York: Washington Square Press.

Note that "The" is capitalized following the colon within the title, and that "Dante" is capitalized because it is a proper noun.

A Chapter that Is Part of an Anthology or Collection

Updike, J. (1982). A&P. In James E. Pickering (Ed.), *Fiction 100* (pp. 1086–1089). New York: Macmillan.

The APA References Page: Periodicals

Article in a Journal with Continuous Pagination

Thomas, J. (1992). How can we reduce the federal deficit? *Journal of Economics, 12,* 22–24.

The number following the title is the volume number. Notice that it is underlined. Note also that commas separate the journal title, volume number, and page numbers.

Article in a Journal Paginated Separately in Each Issue

Seaforth, P. (1983). The role of television in presidential elections. *Journal of American Politics, 6*(4), 19–23.

In this case you follow the volume number "6" with the issue number (4) which is placed in parentheses.

General Interest Magazines

General interest magazines, which are frequently published either monthly or weekly, cite the date of publication, rather than the volume number. The following example illustrates the correct format for magazines that are published monthly.

Barker, J. R. (1989, April). Living with a pit bull and loving it. *The Canine Courier,* pp. 26–29.

If a magazine or newspaper does not indicate the name of the author, begin with the title of the article as shown below. This example also illustrates the correct date format for magazines that are published weekly.

Chaos in television. (1979, March 12). *Time,* pp. 60–61.

Newspapers

For a newspaper entry, provide the author's name, the title of the article, the name of the newspaper as it appears on the front page and the complete date (year, month and day). Page numbers should be listed using the numbering format actually used by the newspaper:

James, N. (1984, Jan. 22). The comedian everyone loves to hate. *The New York Times,* p. 23.

In this example, "The" is part of the name of *The New York Times.* In many cases (e.g., *Los Angeles Times*), "The" is not part of the newspaper's name and would not be included in the citation.

The APA Style: Other Types of Sources

Personal Communications and Interviews

Under the APA system, personal communications such as letters, memos, and telephone conversations are *not* entered in the reference list but are cited in the body of the paper:

James Kohl (personal communication, June 20, 1990) indicated that...

However, published interviews are cited and are listed on the References page. Use the format appropriate for the published source of the interview. The following is an example of an interview published in a monthly magazine.

Smith, J. (1988, May). [Interview with Thomas Mason, Predictions for the eighties]. *Futurist*, pp. 16, 38–40.

Note the correct format for citing discontinuous pages as shown in the previous example.

Electronic Databases

Online databases of publications (such as LexisNexis, PsycINFO, ProQuest, Expanded Academic, and Ovid) are cited the same as a printed source, but with the following modifications: the phrase "Electronic version" appears in square brackets after the title; the citation ends with the word "Retrieved" followed by the date of access, the word "from" followed by the name of the electronic database, and finally the word "database." Here are some examples:

Murray, E. (2004, December 4). New questions about vitamin E [Electronic version]. *Los Angeles Times,* B4. Retrieved May 15, 2005, from Lexis-Nexis database.

Debier, C., Ylitalo, G. M., Weise, M., Gulland, F., Costa, D.P., Le Boeuf, B. J., De Tillesse, T., & Larondelle, Y. (2005). PCBs and DDT in the serum of juvenile California sea lions: associations with vitamins A and E and thyroid hormones [Electronic version]. *Environmental Pollution,* 134(2), 323–332. Retrieved May 12, 2005, from PsycINFO database.

The APA References Page: The Internet

When you cite an online source, APA guidelines recommend including as much of the following identifying information as possible:

> Author's name or authors' names

> Date of online publication or most recent update

> Title of document

> Title of periodical, in italics

> Date of retrieval or download

> Electronic address (URL)

Below are sample citations for different kinds of sources found on the World Wide Web:

Article in an Online Academic or Professional Journal

Petitti, D. B. (2005). Some surprises, some answers, and more questions about hormone therapy [Electronic version]. *Journal of the American Medical Association, 294,* 245–246. Retrieved June 15, 2005, from http://jama.ama-assn.org/cgi/content/full/294/2/245

Scholarly Paper

Wallace, H. E. (2005). Woman's education according to Rousseau and Wollstonecraft. *Feminism and Women's Studies.* Retrieved June 4, 2005, from http://feminism.eserver.org/theory/papers/womens-education.txt

Report

Hickson, A. (2005). Analytical review: Manitoba Public Insurance Corporation motorcycle risk study. University of Manitoba Transport Institute. Retrieved July 7, 2005, from http://www.umti.ca/Documents/496/Analytical%20review%20final%20all%20edits1.pdf

Article in an Online Encyclopedia, Dictionary or Other Reference

Baaba Maal. (1998). *African Music Encyclopedia.* Retrieved March 17, 2005, from http://africanmusic.org/artists/maal.html

Abstract

Tarnopolsky, M. A., Atkinson, S. A., Phillips, S. M., & MacDougall, J. D. (1995). Carbohydrate loading and metabolism during exercise in men and women. *Journal of Applied Physiology, 78,* 1360–1368. Abstract retrieved January 22, 2005, from http://www-rohan.sdsu.edu/dept/coachsci/csa/vol23/tarnopol.htm

U.S. Government Report Available Online

Bureau of Justice Assistance. (2004). Project safe neighborhoods: America's network against gun violence. Retrieved August 6, 2005, from http://www.ncjrs.org/pdffiles1/bja/205263.pdf

Article in an Online Magazine

Epstein, J. (2005, July 11). Romancing the hedge funds: Hollywood's new golden goose. *Slate.* Retrieved August 22, 2005, from http://slate.msn.com/id/2122399/

Article in an Online Newspaper

Guan, X. (2005, July 18). Panda leaves wild for wander in city centre. *China Daily.* Retrieved August 1, 2005, from http://www.chinadaily.com.cn/english/doc/2005-07/18/content_461005.htm

Professional Site

Treating Type 2 diabetes with dietary supplements. (2005). National Center for Complementary and Alternative Medicine. Retrieved February 2, 2005, from http://nccam.nih.gov/health/diabetes/

Personal Site

Sullivan, A. (2002). The Camille Paglia Interview. Retrieved March 17, 2005, from http://www.andrewsullivan.com/interviews.php

Sample "References" Page in APA Style

Here is an example of a References page. The left, right, top, and bottom margins should all be 1.5 inches in the APA format. All text is double-spaced. The reference list should only contain works cited in the text; the text citation and Reference page entry must be identical.

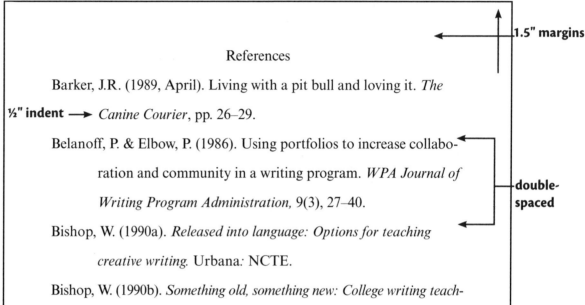

References

Barker, J.R. (1989, April). Living with a pit bull and loving it. *The Canine Courier*, pp. 26–29.

Belanoff, P. & Elbow, P. (1986). Using portfolios to increase collaboration and community in a writing program. *WPA Journal of Writing Program Administration*, 9(3), 27–40.

Bishop, W. (1990a). *Released into language: Options for teaching creative writing*. Urbana: NCTE.

Bishop, W. (1990b). *Something old, something new: College writing teachers and classroom change*. Carbondale: Southern Illinois UP.

Chaos in Television. (1979, March 12). *Time*, pp. 60–61.

Diederich, P. (1974). *Measuring growth in English*. Urbana: NCTE.

Gardner, H. (1983). *Frames of mind: The theory of multiple intelligence*s. New York: Basic.

James, N. (1984, January 22). The comedian everyone loves to hate. *The New York Times*, p. 23.

Kirschenbaum, H., Simon S., & Napier, R. (1971). *Wad-ja-get? The grading game in American education*. New York: Hart Publishing.

Seaforth, P. (1983). The Role of Television in Presidential Elections. *Journal of American Politics*, 6(4), 19–23.

Thomas, J. (1989). How can we reduce the federal deficit? *Journal of Economics*, 12, 22–24.

1.5" margins

double-spaced

½" indent →

Part

STUDENT GUIDE TO WRITING 150

Writing 150 Course Features and Requirements

Because Writing 150 sections are oriented around thematic groups (e.g., "Technology and Social Change," "Education and Intellectual Development," etc.), writing sections will necessarily exhibit considerable diversity, particularly in terms of the topics for writing projects. Each Writing 150 section will also have a unique character because of the individuality and teaching style of the instructor, since the Writing Program has found that writing instruction is most effective when instructors are encouraged to employ individual initiative and creativity.

But these necessary and beneficial diversities arise from a fundamental integrity of curriculum and pedagogy. Whatever the thematic or whoever the instructor, all Writing 150 sections share a number of common features and requirements.

Writing Requirements

Writing Projects: Writing 150 requires you to complete four papers written in response to four separate and distinct writing projects. Your instructor will provide you with an assignment sheet defining the specific expectations for each essay, including the purpose and context of the writing project, the suggested length, the due date, and the specific writing task.

The first three assignments will afford you the opportunity to survey and explore issues, concepts, and theoretical perspectives relevant to the Writing 150 theme in which you are enrolled. In many cases, they will be sequenced so that later assignments may make use of information provided in earlier assignments and so that the three assignments together provide a conceptual and theoretical foundation for the culminating fourth assignment.

Final Portfolio: The final portfolio consists of the culminating fourth assignment and pertinent ancillary materials that provide scaffolding for the assignment (such as a project proposals, opinion pieces, journal entries).

The fourth assignment, in particular, will ask you to select, with the approval of your instructor, an issue pertinent to your Writing 150 theme. Then, drawing upon the conceptual foundation provided in the earlier assignments, you will use this issue to compose an essay addressing the fundamental and most general critical question of "What is to be done?" While this final assignment will certainly make use of additional research, it will not be an "information dump," but rather an opportunity for you to grapple with key dimensions—personal, conceptual, political, and socio-cultural—of the theme which Writing 150 has addressed and which you have explored in the first three assignments.

Ancillary Writing Activities: Over the course of the semester you will be asked to complete a number of informal writing tasks in response to readings, in support of writing projects, or as part of workshop or conference lessons and activities. The majority of ancillary writing will be directly related to the assignment and thus will provide a means to keep you on pace and to prepare you for class discussions and activities.

Such writing might take a number of forms, including, but not limited to: journal entries, editorials, peer critique, and reflective writing following the submission of an essay. Regardless of the form it takes, the primary function is to provide you with a venue in which to experience the epistemic power of writing—the way in which writing not only records ideas but, in so doing, serves to generate new ones.

Consulting with Your Instructor

Conferences: To provide a greater degree of individualized attention, your instructor will arrange four conferences with you over the course of the semester. Some of these may be one-to-one conferences, others small-group conferences of two to four students. Because each set of individual conferences requires five to seven total hours of time, your instructor will normally cancel one office hour and half of the class meeting time (seventy-five of one-hundred-fifty minutes) during weeks when conferences are being held.

Office Hours: If you have questions or concerns that cannot be addressed during classroom or conference meetings (or before or after class), please feel free to take advantage of your instructor's office hours. Two hours will be scheduled each week in which conferences are not being held; during weeks with conferences, one office hour will be scheduled with the other usually being used as part of the conference hours. Your instructor's course outline will list the time and place for the office hours arranged for your section.

Attendance and Participation

Attendance Requirements: Good attendance has particular importance to a writing class. Writing is an activity—it's something you do, not just something you can "catch-up on" at a later date—and to develop as a writer you need to engage in a number of activities and interactions with other writers. To encourage as much participation and practice as possible, Writing 150 is taught primarily in a workshop and conference format rather than in a lecture setting. Consistent attendance is therefore important both to your own progress in Writing 150 and to the effective functioning of the class to which you belong. Absences disrupt not only your own learning experience but also the teamwork and interaction upon which a writing workshop depends. For this reason, excessive absences will affect your grade in two important ways. The direct result of absences is to lower your marks for participation, which counts for 5% of your overall grade. The indirect effect of absences is even greater, however, since absences usually result in weaker papers and often lead to late penalties and missing work. Indeed, if your cumulative absences exceed a total of three weeks or more, it is unlikely that you will be able to derive full benefit from the course. Most seriously of all, if your absences reach the point at which you can no longer derive adequate benefit from the class, you will be required to withdraw from the course and complete it at a future date when you will be able to attend—and to avoid receiving an "F."

Here is a description of how some of these direct and indirect consequences of absences may have an effect on class performance:

> Absences totaling less than one week of classes (two absences for TTh and MW sections; three meetings for MWF sections), will undoubtedly incur some of the indirect consequences described above, even if there is no direct penalty for the number of absences.

> Absences totaling more than one week's worth of meetings will result in a direct penalty of up to 5% of the final mark, together with additional indirect effects on that grade.

> Absences totaling more than two weeks' worth of meetings will usually undermine the participation mark and lower the grades given to a number of assignments, thus resulting in a severe reduction in the final grade.

> Students who accumulate three weeks' worth of absences (20% of class time)—for any reason—will fail the course.

> Absence from a scheduled conference is equivalent to absence from class.

If you will miss class to participate in a **university-sponsored activity**, you are responsible for informing your instructor in writing at least one week before the impending absence. Notification should include the name and phone number of the sponsoring university agency and/or representative. At your instructor's discretion, you may be required to submit in advance work scheduled for submission on the day of your absence.

If a **medical or personal** emergency or the **observance of a religious holiday** causes you to miss class, you are responsible for notifying your instructor in advance and for arranging to make up any work you will miss. When emergency conditions preclude advanced notification, you should email your instructor as soon as reasonably possible.

Because even notified or "excused" absences interfere with your learning, you are responsible for ensuring that your total number of absences does not exceed the threshold figures described previously.

Attendance and University Withdrawal Policies: There will be important dates you should be aware of if you find yourself struggling with your attendance for any reason (including ailments, university activities, or personal concerns). While the specific dates will change each semester, students should understand that semesters are divided into four periods: Weeks 1–3, Weeks 4–7, Weeks 8–12, and Weeks 13–on. Below are the outcomes a student might expect in connection to attendance (without regard to the quality of any completed work):

PERIOD (WEEKS)	ATTENDANCE SITUATION	OUTCOME
Weeks 1–3	Student May Add/Drop	No Indication on Transcript
Weeks 4–7	Student May Drop	No "W" on Transcript but Tuition Fees Apply
Weeks 8–12	Student May Withdraw	"W" on Transcript/No GPA Affect
Weeks 13–on	Student May Not Withdraw If Student Does Not Attend and/or Substantially Participate in Previous Weeks	"UW" 0.0 Value Calculated into GPA

During the first three weeks, students may withdraw from a class without a "W" on their transcripts. During weeks 4–7, if students withdraw from class, they will not receive an automatic grade of "W" for the course, but there will be some tuition fees associated with such a withdrawal. If a student withdraws from a class within Weeks 8–12, a "W" will appear on the student's transcript. The withdrawal, however, does not affect the student's cumulative GPA. If a student, however, does not drop the course, but also does not *substantially participate* (in all of the ways described above) throughout the term up to and including the 12th week, the instructor marks the student's grade as a "UW" (*unofficial* withdrawal). Unlike an *official* withdrawal, a "UW" is calculated into a student's GPA, and carries a value of 0.0.

Students are not permitted to withdraw from a course after Week 12; however, if a student faces a sudden health or family emergency the student may ask for an incomplete ("IN") in the course. Incompletes are solely reserved for students whose work had been up to date prior to the emergency and for situations in which the student submits adequate documentation to support the claim. Students must discuss the option of an "IN" grade with the course instructor who must then fill out and sign a contract specifying the work remaining and a timetable for its completion (a maximum of one year). If the student does not complete the course within a year, the grade turns into an "IX," which is the equivalent of an "F" in terms of the student's GPA.

Your instructor's course outline will explain how these penalties will be assessed in your section, but the basic message is simple: you should not miss a class or a conference for any reason other than a medical or personal emergency.

Participation in Classes and Conferences: A writing course requires the active participation of all students as well as the instructor. You will be expected to come to class or conferences fully prepared and ready to work. Participation also implies a willingness to engage in dialogue—to listen tolerantly to the ideas of others, to offer criticism in a spirit of helpfulness and goodwill, and to allow your own arguments and opinions to be criticized in turn.

Grade Weighting in Writing 150

The evaluation of your writing will follow the Grading and Evaluation Rubric. Because of the developmental nature of a *praxis* course such as Writing 150, grades will be weighted so as to give greater weight to later assignments. The provisional grading allotments (which may slightly change to reflect circumstances arising during the semester) are as follows:

Participation	**5 %**
Writing Project 1–3	**45 %**
Writing Project 4 and Final Portfolio	**35 %**
Ancillary Writing Activities	**15 %**

Your Responsibilities

Your chief task in Writing 150 is to improve your ability to produce clear, thoughtful, and effective academic writing; closely allied to this is the need to become more familiar with the expectations and commitments of the academic discourse community. In order to successfully achieve these objectives, you need to participate fully in the learning process throughout the semester. Keep in mind the following responsibilities:

Understanding Requirements: : Your first responsibility is to understand the policies and standards that govern the course, both as outlined in this document and set forth in your instructor's syllabus. As the semester progresses, keep track of all assignments, reading tasks, due dates, and conference appointments. If any information strikes you as unclear or incomplete, ask your instructor for clarification.

Time Management: University guidelines suggest that in order to make satisfactory academic progress students should set aside two hours per unit per week for study time. You should plan to spend, on average, eight hours per week completing writing and reading assignments for your Writing 150 class.

You are responsible for managing your calendar and your obligations in such a way as to allow yourself sufficient time for writing. Remember that as the due date approaches writers almost never wish they had less time for a project but almost always wish they had more. Begin your writing process as soon as you receive the writing project, work on your project for an hour or two at least every other day, and read through your developing draft every day in order to retain familiarity with it; never leave anything other than final proofreading for the day before the paper is due.

Don't Miss Classes or Conferences: You are responsible for your own attendance and for dealing with the consequences of any absences. If you must be absent to participate in a university-sponsored event, you must inform your instructor at least a week in advance of the absence and, if your instructor requests it, submit in advance any work due on the date of your planned absence. If you have a medical or personal emergency, or if you are observing a religious holiday, it is your responsibility to notify your instructor as soon as possible and to arrange to make up any work you have missed or will miss.

Participate Responsibly in Class: A successful writing workshop depends not simply upon the activities of the instructor, but also upon the participation and contributions of all other class members. Behave toward your classmates with the same maturity, respect, and thoughtfulness that you would wish to convey in your writing. Seek neither to monopolize nor to evade classroom or group discussions. In sharing and critiquing writing, try to extend to the writing of others the tolerance, thoroughness, and constructive analysis that you would want your own writing to receive.

Provide Full Documentation of Your Writing Process: Submission of the following materials is required for each writing project:

> **All prewriting materials,** including invention and heuristic exercises, notes, points-to-make lists, and rough plans.

> **A sequence of hardcopy drafts.** As you draft and revise your paper, print off copies of your evolving essay at several stages during the revision process and save a separate copy of each significant draft on your computer.

These procedures will provide both you and your instructor with a thorough overview of your writing process, which can help you discover ways to make that process increasingly effective.

In addition, you should consider the benefits of "marking-up" drafts by hand, a practice that most writers find essential during the revision process. A computer screen allows you to see only a small portion of a multi-page text, and it doesn't allow you to get as "close" to your text as you can through handwritten revisions that allow you to insert words and shift phrases in a provisional manner that doesn't overwrite and efface the prior draft. These changes can then be introduced into a new copy of the revised draft to begin the next stage of revision.

If you're doing a thorough job of revision, you should be able to save and print off *at least* two significant rough drafts to submit with your final presentation draft.

Submit Work on Time: Writing projects are due when called for in class and may be penalized if not submitted at that time. If you anticipate that you will be unable to submit a writing project when due, notify your instructor *in advance* either through e-mail or by leaving a message with the Writing Program office (213-740-1980). If you wish to submit a late paper and cannot locate your instructor, bring the paper to the Writing Program office (JEF 150) where it will be logged in (thus protecting you by providing an official record of the paper's submission) and placed in your instructor's mailbox. Never submit a late paper by leaving it in the classroom, placing it on your instructor's desk, or leaving it anywhere else than at the front desk of the Writing Program office.

Be Responsible for Your Own Authority: The term *authority* derives from the term *author.* As a writer, you have authority and must take responsibility for whatever you write.

This means, first of all, that in your writing you should assert and argue what you genuinely believe to be true; you cannot exercise responsible authority by taking positions you don't believe in. Keep in mind that Writing 150 is a course in rhetoric, and that rhetoric, by definition, deals with issues for which there are a variety of possible positions and no clear-cut "right" answer (as, for example, there might be in a math class). Note that your authority as a writer does not give you license to make unsupported assertions, to argue deceptively, or to ignore the countervailing claims and reasoning of others; on the contrary, responsible authority is characterized by careful reasoning, thorough support, and honest and good-willed engagement with opposing viewpoints.

In addition, of course, being responsible for your authority as a writer also means conscientiously ensuring that that authority is never over-written by someone else's, either intentionally or accidentally. Plagiarism, for example, not only insults the authority of the writer whose work is pilfered but forfeits (and, if the plagiarism is discovered, destroys) the authority and reputation of the writer who misappropriated the material. An even more difficult problem of authority is raised when you receive assistance with your writing. The Writing Program encourages collaboration with your instructor, with Writing Center consultants, and with your classmates; such interactions constitute one of the most important and effective means by which writing is taught. In undertaking collaborative interactions, however, remember that you are finally responsible for guaranteeing that the resulting text represents your abilities and authority and not those of the persons assisting you, however well-meaning they may be. A simple guideline may help: *Never allow someone else to construct a section of your text longer than one or two sentences that you would not be able to produce on your own, and never allow anyone to copyedit more than the first page of your paper.*

Take Responsibility for Your Education: Don't let problems fester. If you feel an issue or question is interfering with your progress in Writing 150, do not remain silent. It is your responsibility to raise the issue with your instructor. This should be done at an appropriate time and place (outside of class or during office hours) and in an appropriate manner (one directed at resolution rather than confrontation). If after discussing the problem with your instructor the situation remains unresolved, call the Writing Program at 213-740-1980 to arrange an appointment with one of the program directors.

Diagnosis, Response, and Evaluation

The Relationship of Diagnosis, Response, and Evaluation

In the Writing Program, commentary upon student writing involves three distinct but related activities:

Diagnosis refers to the *analysis* of student essays as product. It has the objective of identifying and assigning relative priority to the text's strengths and weaknesses. It does not involve comparing, ranking, or grading.

Response is an *interaction* between the instructor and the student about the text, the writing process, and the student's developing abilities and understanding as a writer. Response goes beyond diagnosis in placing the text's strengths and weaknesses within an explanatory framework that will help the student identify ways to improve his or her overall competence as a writer.

Evaluation is a process of *assessment* that judges student writing in relation to program standards and in comparison with other student texts. Evaluation is exclusively concerned with the qualities of the text as *product*. For reasons that will be discussed below, your instructor will not attempt to evaluate your writing process. In the program, evaluation is to a large extent a collaborative activity carried out by groups of instructors (as, for example, in evaluating the final portfolios), but individual instructors are responsible for the evaluation of assignments not included in portfolios and for assigning semester grades that reflect program standards and the judgment of the portfolio assessment groups.

Issues in Evaluation/Grading

Most of this section of the *Student Guide* discusses matters of diagnosis and response, since these are important to your development as a writer. But evaluation is a reality, and all Writing Program instructors share in the responsibility to ensure that students are graded in a consistent and legitimate manner.

In this regard, it is important not to confuse matters of process and product. Not only is the writing process extremely difficult to observe in its entirety, but no standards exist to gauge its effectiveness except for those that are applied to the resulting product. For these reasons, the instructional approach within the Writing Program is to "teach process but grade product." Except in cases of plagiarism or illegitimate collaboration, the process whereby a text is created should not be graded in itself nor should it influence the grade that the text would otherwise receive on its own merits.

Students should keep the following points in mind with regard to evaluation:

> During the writing process, instructors "coach" students to help them develop their skills as writers. However, they must eventually "judge" their students' work, an activity very different than coaching.

> Portfolio evaluation is designed to reduce the conflict between the coaching a student receives during the writing process and the judgment of the final product. It also helps increase the reliability and validity of grading decisions by providing an inter-subjective dimension to the evaluation process.

> To improve what you produce as a writer, you must change and improve what you *do* when you write. Simply memorizing rules or learning rhetorical principles is not enough. Instead, you will need to commit time and effort to practicing various ways to develop ideas, to arrange these into a rough draft, and to revise this draft until it achieves your purpose.

> Although there is a positive correlation between the time and effort you spend and the quality of your writing, grades are not awarded directly on the basis of effort.

> The analytic terms adopted by Writing Program instructors to diagnose and respond to the quality of your writing and the criteria of the general evaluation rubric both emphasize thoughtful, critical analysis of topics and issues. Although papers with numerous errors in grammar and mechanics will receive lower grades, grammatical correctness is expected in college and is not, therefore, rewarded in itself.

Analytical Terms for Use in Diagnosis, Response, and Evaluation

In order to explain both the strengths of your papers as well as what you may do to improve your writing, it is helpful to have a concise set of analytical or descriptive terms that can be used to discuss important dimensions of a text. With time, all writers develop a vocabulary suited to this purpose, and the six terms described below are not offered as being unique or original—they are likely to be synonyms for terms you may already use to discuss writing. However, these terms reflect most of the qualities defined in the Writing Program grading standards. They can therefore serve both as a common vocabulary relating the diagnosis of texts to an explanatory response and as a basis for evaluation.

These terms describe important characteristics of all university-level writing.

COGENCY (ARGUMENTATIVE FORCE OR ANALYTICAL INSIGHT)	ADDRESSING THE ISSUE(S)
The insight and vitality of the concepts underlying the paper's argument or analysis.	*The extent to which the paper explores the issue(s) set forth in the assignment and addresses all aspects of the writing task.*
Strong: Paper's argument or analysis is insightful, vigorous, and potentially compelling.	**Strong:** The paper addresses the assignment in depth, thoroughly exploring the complexities of the issue(s).
Acceptable: Paper's argument or analysis is plausible, clear, and consistent.	**Acceptable:** The paper addresses the assignment and recognizes the complexities of the issue(s).
Weak: Paper's argument or analysis is implausible, unclear, incomplete, or inconsistent.	**Weak:** The paper treats the assignment in a superficial, simplistic, or disjointed manner.
SUPPORT	STYLE
The extent to which the paper's assertions are supported with examples, evidence, or reasoning that are appropriate for the intended audience.	*The effectiveness of the paper's sentence structure, word choice, fluency, and tone in terms of its purpose and intended audience.*
Strong: The paper's argument or analysis receives judicious, full, and convincing support.	**Strong:** The sentence structure, word choice, fluency, and tone of the paper enhance its effectiveness and reinforce its purpose.
Acceptable: The argument or analysis receives credible support.	**Acceptable:** The sentence structure, word choice, fluency, and tone of the paper contribute to its effectiveness and adequately support its purpose.
Weak: The argument or analysis receives inadequate, unconvincing, or irrelevant support.	**Weak:** The sentence structure, word choice, fluency, and tone of the paper detract from its effectiveness or are inappropriate to its purpose.
CONTROL	GRAMMAR AND MECHANICS
The organizational quality of the paper, both in terms of its overall structure and of its individual paragraphs.	*The quality of the paper at the surface level: syntax, grammar, spelling, punctuation, and format.*
Strong: The paper is well structured; its form at all levels contributes to its purpose.	**Strong:** The paper is nearly impeccable in its syntax, grammar, spelling, punctuation, and format.
Acceptable: The paper is generally well-structured, with few flaws in its overall organization or its paragraphing.	**Acceptable:** Sentence-level errors do not seriously detract from the paper's effectiveness.
Weak: The paper is poorly structured; organizational flaws undermine its effectiveness.	**Weak:** Sentence-level errors are so frequent and disruptive as to detract from the paper's effectiveness.

Writing 150: Writing Program General Evaluation Rubric

The following rubric outlines the general criteria used to assign grades in Writing Program courses. The + and – grades allow instructors to make finer qualitative distinctions concerning their students' ability at each grade point; A+ and F are not recognized by the University.

In general, thoughtful, critical essays are rewarded. Those which demonstrate overall organizational and argumentative/analytical skills will usually be rewarded over those which merely demonstrate sentence-level competence. Those which fail to respond to all aspects of the assignment will usually not receive a passing grade.

In evaluating an essay, the reader will first make a **C/D** decision. After having made this initial judgment, the reader then decides whether essays falling above this cut deserve to be raised beyond the **C** range to the **B** or **A** level, and whether essays falling below this cut should be lowered from the **D** range to **F**.

Features of A and B Writing

A WRITING *is exceptionally well conceived, developed, organized, and expressed. It will:*

Present a cogent and insightful argument/analysis. The author responds to the assignment in a consistently forceful manner that is not only thoughtful, but also thought-provoking. The writing is often distinguished by intellectual curiosity, original insights, measured skepticism of received claims, and a willingness to engage in a careful consideration of genuine issues. The essay is marked by intellectual and structural cogency.

Provide compelling support for the overall argument/analysis. The argument or analysis receives full (and fully convincing) support: the author includes enough judiciously-chosen materials or details to emphatically support what he or she is trying to do. When the author employs sources, he or she is critical and confident concerning their use, and employs them to further his or her own authority and point of view.

Develop its argument or analysis with organizational clarity and logical force. The author controls the writer-reader transaction both explicitly and implicitly, seamlessly maintaining the reader's engagement with and attention to the argument or analysis throughout the work.

Demonstrate sophisticated exploration of the issue(s) set forth in the assignment. The author is able to negotiate the complexities of the issue(s) raised in a provocative, controlled manner. The author fully responds to the writing task, demonstrating a mature knowledge about the subject and a judicious sense of its impact on the reader. The paper is often marked by the integration and synthesis of relevant theories and pertinent concepts.

Employ a style that reinforces the paper's effectiveness and advances its purpose within the context of the academic discourse community.

Display maturity in sentence variety, grammar, spelling, and usage. Surface errors are virtually non-existent; the reader is left free to enjoy the author's style and tone and the intellectual force of the writing.

B WRITING *offers a consistently strong response to the assignment. It will:*

Present a clear, principled argument/analysis. The author responds to the assignment in a direct, thoughtful, and sometimes forceful manner; the paper demonstrates a strong and consistent point of view.

Use effective examples and reasoning to support the overall argument/analysis. The argument or analysis receives relevant support; the author includes enough well-chosen materials or details to support what he or she is trying to do. If sources are used, the author incorporates them to further his or her own authority and point of view.

Display strong overall organization, paragraph development, and logical transition. The author demonstrates a good sense of structural control: the paper's form directly contributes to its purpose; transitions are purposeful. The author directs the reader's attention through the unfolding work.

Purposefully address and explore the issue(s) set forth in the assignment. The paper responds to the writing task and explores the complexities of the issue(s) raised. The author demonstrates reliable knowledge about the subject and good sense about its impact on the reader.

Employ a style that is appropriate and furthers the purpose of the paper. The author has developed good control over (if not mastery of) academic discourse.

Display strength in sentence variety, grammar, spelling, and usage. Surface errors are infrequent and inconsequential: the reader is left free to consider global matters, hardly ever distracted by surface matters. The author's meaning is always clear.

The C/D Distinction

C WRITING *will generally demonstrate the competence expected of college-level writing and reasoning while exhibiting certain shortcomings. It will:*

Offer a sometimes competent but often limited argument/analysis in response to the assignment. The argument or analysis is plausible, relatively clear, and generally consistent, but may be derivative (lacking originality) or too self-centered (lacking the context and perspective necessary in academic writing).

Use credible but sometimes undeveloped or problematic examples and reasoning to support the argument/analysis. The author includes enough material or detail to support what he or she is trying to do, but tends to overlook important or relevant evidence. When required, secondary sources are properly cited but may be handled awkwardly or in a manner that displaces or overshadows the student's own argument.

Display competence in overall organization, paragraph development, and logical transition, even if it occasionally exhibits organizational or argumentative/analytical weaknesses. The author generally demonstrates structural control (the readers most often know where they're being taken and why), but sometimes fails to properly cue readers (e.g., by employing weak paragraph transitions).

Address the issue(s) set forth in the assignment. The paper responds to the writing task but may fall short of adequately recognizing the complexities of the issue(s) raised in the assignment. Nonetheless, the author does not just go through the motions, but cares about his or her subject and its impact on the reader.

Use a style and tone appropriate to the purpose. The language aims to support the author's purpose but may fall short of the expectations for essay writing within the academic community.

Display general competence in sentence variety, grammar, spelling, and usage. Occasional surface errors may detract from the paper's purpose but they do not significantly interfere with the reader's comprehension of the essay.

D WRITING *will offer a limited argument/analysis in response to the assignment wherein short-comings largely outweigh the positive qualities of the writing. It will be marked by several of the following weaknesses:*

An implausible, unclear, incomplete, or inconsistent argument or analysis. The paper lacks the cogency and purpose necessary for competent college-level writing; the paper fails to exhibit careful thinking.

Inadequate, unconvincing, irrelevant, or derivative support. The paper accumulates (often paragraph by paragraph) derivative and/or anecdotal examples without integrating them into a focused argument/analysis. The author relies on inappropriate—or weak—examples or reasoning to support the overall discussion. If sources are required, the author may piece together writing from secondary sources without using it in the service of his or her own argument or point of view. Alternatively, the author may not include enough material or detail to support the purpose of the paper.

Flaws in organization, paragraph development, or logical transition. The paper lacks structural fluency: organizational flaws cause a lack of overall coherence, undermining the paper's purpose. The reader is too often puzzled by the course the paper takes, or the paper relies too exclusively on formulaic organization, thereby becoming stilted and predictable.

Failure to seriously or thoughtfully address the issue(s) set forth in the assignment. The paper treats the issue(s) simplistically; the argument/analysis generally overlooks the complexity of the issue(s) raised. The author doesn't care enough about the subject or the reader's expectations, and may fail to respond to all aspects of the writing task.

An inappropriate style or tone. The style and tone detract from the purpose and are inappropriate in terms of the academic discourse community.

Flaws in syntax, grammar, usage, or spelling. Mechanical errors detract from the paper's purpose or interfere with the reader's comprehension. Significant problems in wording or syntax make the writing unclear or confusing.

F WRITING *will compound the weaknesses of D writing, to the point that the paper seems beyond the scope of the normal revision process. Specifically, F writing will:*

Fail to recognize or adequately respond to the writing task.
Be far too general or present a vacuous discussion of the issue.
Rely on remarkably weak or inappropriate examples.
Have little controlling organization or logical coherence.
Have serious and extensive flaws in syntax, grammar, or usage.

Course Policies

Final Course Portfolios

In lieu of a final examination, the Writing Program uses a system of portfolio evaluation to assess the proficiency of students as they complete Writing 150. This approach not only allows students to present their strongest work for final evaluation but also helps to ensure a more valid and equitable grading process. The mark given your portfolio will count as 35% of your semester grade.

Your Final Portfolio consists of Writing Project 4 and a set of pertinent ancillary materials that provide scaffolding for WP4. Because your portfolio is meant to represent your best work as a writer, it follows that portfolios are evaluated according to the most rigorous standards of the grading rubric.

Portfolio Procedures and Format

Portfolio Submissions: On the date specified by your instructor, you must submit an unmarked final-draft copy of Writing Project 4. The paper must be identified with your name, the course name and section number, your instructor's name, the date, and the writing project number:

Your Name
Instructor's Name
Writing 150—Section #
Date
Writing Project #

Because portfolios are evaluated in a collaborative grading session on the first Stop Day after the end of classes, late portfolios cannot be accepted. Your instructor will specify the date on which portfolios are due, and any student failing to meet this deadline is subject to receiving an **F** as his or her portfolio mark. Students who otherwise qualify for an **INcomplete** will be required to submit their portfolio directly to the program when making up the **IN**.

To be eligible to submit a portfolio, students on the submission date must be maintaining a grade higher than **F**. Any student who is missing more than one assignment is ineligible to submit the portfolio and will receive an **F** for the course.

Portfolio Evaluation

During portfolio grading your instructor collaborates with other instructors in the Writing Program. Collaborative grading permits a more valid and equitable assessment of writing because it relies upon the opinion of more than one reader. Essays are not ball bearings, and cannot be measured in a strictly "objective" fashion; any assessment of writing involves some degree of subjectivity. But this does not imply that writing cannot be evaluated in a manner that is consistent and fair, and collaborative grading contributes in this regard by requiring *inter*-subjective agreement: if a paper receives widely divergent marks from two readers, it is given additional readings until a fair and appropriate mark can be agreed upon.

The grade calibration provided through portfolio evaluation is particularly important in a program that is based on dialogic pedagogy and that encourages conferences and other direct interaction between instructors and individual students. After coaching a student's writing for fifteen weeks, an instructor can find it very difficult to switch roles and become the judge of that writing. The collaborative grading process helps in two ways, by providing the instructor with an outside perspective and by in turn permitting the instructor to survey the writing ability of students in other sections of Writing 150. This sort of double calibration helps to make evaluation within and across different sections of Writing 150 as fair and consistent as possible. Keep in mind, however, that collaborative grading serves an advisory function, and that your instructor has final responsibility for assigning the ultimate portfolio mark and for determining your semester grade.

Grade Appeals

The *USC Catalogue* states that "The teacher's evaluation of each individual student is the final basis for assigning grades." However, the university has established an appeals procedure to protect students against "prejudiced or capricious academic evaluation."

As noted in *SCampus*, the grade appeals procedure in the Writing Program differs somewhat from—and supersedes—the general University and College of Letters, Arts and Sciences procedures for disputed academic evaluation. The Writing Program director decides appeals at the program level. All appeals involving the reevaluation of a student's work will be initially referred to an advisory committee of experienced instructors to obtain an independent evaluation of the work before making a final decision. This procedure replicates the program's use of collaborative evaluation for the final portfolios, a method designed to ensure the integrity and consistency of grading standards throughout the program.

Because careful review of a semester's work in writing is time-consuming, we ask students to file their appeals as early as possible, but *no later than the end of the semester (excluding the summer session) following the one in which the student completed the course*.

Writing Program Appeals Procedures

1. Consult your instructor about the grade in question. If a mathematical error has been made in calculating the semester mark, your instructor will submit a memo to the Director of the Writing Program explaining the error and requesting that the grade be changed.

2. If the requested grade change requires your instructor to reevaluate the quality of the writing in your essays or to reconsider the weight given to other aspects of your work in the class, you must submit a formal grade appeal.

3. To appeal your grade, assemble a portfolio of all essays written for the class, including your final portfolio, any in-class essays, and the drafts and final versions of all out-of-class writing. If your instructor is supporting your appeal, request a letter from him or her explaining the reasons why your grade should be changed.

4. Write a letter of appeal that includes the following:

   > Instructor's Name

   > Class Number

   > Student's Name and Address

   > Student's Identification Number

   > A detailed statement explaining the reason for the appeal. Please remember that the grade appeals procedure is designed to protect students from "capricious or prejudiced" evaluation and the burden of proof is on the student to demonstrate that the grade received was unfair.

5. Place your essays and letter of appeal in a manila envelope and mail or deliver it to the following address:

    Director, Writing Program
    JEF 150
    University of Southern California
    Los Angeles, CA 90089-0022

    ATTN: Grade Appeal

Incompletes

University Policy

You may receive a grade of Incomplete only if you have a documented illness or other emergency that occurs *after the twelfth week of the semester*. If your illness or emergency occurs before the end of the twelfth week, you must withdraw from the course if you will be unable to complete the work and pass the course. This policy is strictly enforced.

For your information, students have the option of purchasing insurance, which will provide a full refund of tuition and fees in the case of a serious illness or accident occurring *before the end of the twelfth week of the semester*. Application forms are available at the Cashier's Office.

Arranging for an Incomplete

Unless it is physically impossible for you to do so, you must arrange for an Incomplete before the final portfolio is graded. Your instructor will fill out a form specifying the work to be done, your grade in the course to date, and the weight the remaining work will carry in determining your final grade.

Removing an Incomplete

According to university policy, you have one year to complete the missing work and remove the Incomplete. To remove the Incomplete, you must complete the missing work and submit it to your instructor for evaluation.

After your instructor evaluates the completed work, the Program will arrange to have your portfolio read by other instructors in the program. Following this portfolio reading, your instructor will assign your semester grade. The Writing Program will then submit a change-of-grade request to the Grade Department. It usually takes about two weeks for the grade change to be processed after it has been submitted.

If you do not complete the missing work and remove the Incomplete by the deadline, you will receive the grade of IX (expired Incomplete), which counts as an F in your grade point average.

Withdrawing from Courses

Official Withdrawals

University policy permits you to withdraw from a course without academic penalty during the first 12 weeks of the semester. If you drop a course during Weeks 1–3, it will not appear on your transcript. If you drop a course during Weeks 4–12, you will receive a grade of **W**. You may not officially withdraw from a course after the 12th week.

Unofficial Withdrawals

If you stop attending a course but remain registered, your instructor will assign a grade of **UW** (unofficial withdrawal). A grade of **UW** counts as an **F** in your grade point average. If you stop attending a course in which you are registered, be sure to drop the course officially.

Course Description

USC Core Writing Requirement

To give you the foundation in academic writing, critical reading, and analytic thinking expected in college-level writing, USC requires that all students complete at least two writing courses.

Most students entering USC complete two semester courses to fulfill this writing requirement: at the freshman level Writing and Critical Reasoning - Thematic Approaches (Writing 150) and an advanced writing course (Writing 340) generally taken during the student's junior year at USC. In addition, on the basis of a placement examination administered at USC, certain students are required to complete an introductory course prior to enrolling in 150, either Introduction to College Writing (Writing 120) or Introduction to College Writing in a Second Language (Writing 121), the companion course for non-native speakers of English.

Writing 150: Writing and Critical Reasoning—Thematic Approaches

Writing 150 introduces the rhetorical techniques good writers need to produce college-level expository prose and helps you apply these strategies to challenging writing tasks, particularly as these involve intertextual argumentation and analysis. Writing 150 focuses on strengthening your ability to interpret and critique information from a variety of sources and to employ that information to advance your own argumentative positions. Writing projects in Writing 150 encourage you to develop sophisticated reading and analytical abilities and to engage issues and ideas drawn from the broad and challenging thematic. You are expected to produce writing that displays closely reasoned argument or analysis, that employs organizational structures appropriate to complex discourse, and that makes use of effectively selected and accurately documented outside sources. In addition, your writing should also show maturity in terms of style, diction, and syntactic fluency. At the conclusion of Writing 150, you should be able to compose an essay of 6–8 pages that explores issues and persuades through reasoned analysis, exhibits sound logic and solid support, incorporates outside sources to advance your own argument, and expresses ideas clearly and concisely.

Prerequisites

To enter Writing 150, you must satisfy one of the following conditions: a combined score of 1100 or higher on the Critical Reading and Writing sections of the SAT (or 24 or higher on the ACT English exam), a score meriting placement into 150 on USC's Composition Proficiency Examination, or completion of Writing 120/121 at USC.

Course Objectives

Writing 150 has four principal objectives, each of which involves a number of other important skills and abilities:

1. **Rhetorical Knowledge and Judgment**

   At the end of Writing 150, you should understand how to:

   › Discover genuine issues and focus on significant purposes in your writing

   › See writing as an interaction between the writer and reader and recognize how to meet the reader's needs

   › Assess different rhetorical situations and respond in a manner that maintains the integrity of your point of view

   › Identify and use conventions appropriate to the rhetorical situation (e.g., citation conventions in various disciplines)

2. **Critical Reasoning and Ethical Inquiry**

   At the end of Writing 150, you should be able to:

   › Use writing as a tool of discovery to facilitate genuine inquiry, creativity, personal learning, independent thinking, and compelling communication

   › Integrate your own ideas with those of others (establishing your own authority while appropriately employing outside sources) to both understand and enter scholarly discussions

   › Interrogate assumptions that underlie personal, social, and cultural beliefs

   › Understand the epistemic and ethical uses of writing and critical reasoning in the creation of meaning and knowledge

3. **The Craft and Processes of Writing**

   At the end of Writing 150, you should:

   › Understand the function of the writing process in terms of creating and completing a successful text

   › Develop multiple tools and flexible strategies for generating, revising, editing, and proofreading texts

   › Understand the collaborative and social aspects of writing processes, but also the individual's responsibility in terms of authorship of the finished product

   › Be able to critique your own and others' works

   › Identify the components of your own writing style while experimenting with diverse styles

4. *Grammatical and Genre Conventions*

At the end of Writing 150, you should:

> ❭ Understand common formats for different kinds of texts

> ❭ Demonstrate knowledge of genre conventions ranging from structure and paragraphing to tone and mechanics

> ❭ Be familiar with the appropriate means of documenting your work

> ❭ Understand the crucial importance of controlling surface features such as syntax, grammar, punctuation, and spelling

Course Requirements

1. Four formal out-of-class essays written in response to *different* assignments. Each essay should be a full 8 typed pages for a total of approximately 8,000 words during the semester and should demonstrate the ability to document sources correctly and to prepare a Works Cited or References page.

2. An in-class diagnostic essay written in response to a previously discussed topic or as prewriting for one of the out-of-class writing projects.

3. Regular informal writing assignments (e.g., responses to readings or class discussions, etc.).

4. A portfolio consisting of Writing Project 4 along with a set of ancillary materials.

5. Research activities in support of argumentative or analytical writing projects.

6. Regular attendance throughout the semester and active participation in class discussions and workshop activities. For a complete explanation of the program's attendance policy, see above.

Academic Integrity

Plagiarism and Illegitimate Assistance

By its very nature, writing involves both individual and collaborative activity. Even when a piece of writing has but one author, that author employs a language system that is shared with others and draws upon ideas and values that are not his or hers alone. Indeed, one of the most important parts of becoming a writer within the academic community is learning how to balance the obligations of individuality and collaboration. As a college writer, you are expected to use writing to develop and assert your own ideas and beliefs—to think for yourself. But at the same time you are expected in college writing to engage the thinking of others, to place your own writing within the context of academic discourse by using or criticizing arguments from that discourse. This double obligation provides a framework in which to discuss two important issues of academic integrity: plagiarism and illegitimate assistance.

Plagiarism

Plagiarism is the unacknowledged and inappropriate use of the ideas or wording of another writer. Plagiarism undermines the intellectual collaboration—the exchange of ideas—that should mark academic discourse because it permits the writer to avoid any genuine involvement with the concepts or opinions of others. Because the false discourse of plagiarism corrupts values to which the university community is fundamentally committed—the pursuit of knowledge, intellectual honesty—plagiarism is considered a grave violation of academic integrity and the sanctions against it are correspondingly severe (see *SCampus*).

Illegitimate Assistance

The obligations to individuality and collaboration can also help to distinguish between legitimate and illegitimate forms of assistance with writing. Legitimate assistance is principally directed at the writing process, at helping to improve the individual writer's abilities rather than at "fixing" any particular paper. Legitimate assistance thus does not intrude upon the writer's obligation to think and write as an individual or upon the obligation to engage the ideas and opinions of others. But illegitimate assistance with writing subverts both obligations. Such assistance is directed not at improving the writer's abilities but at producing a paper that those abilities could not independently achieve. Moreover, such assistance constitutes a fraudulent form of collaboration, one in which the contributions of one participant dominate and conceal the contributions of the other. Illegitimate assistance is thus similar to plagiarism in serving to undermine academic discourse and the intellectual values of the university community.

Avoiding Plagiarism and Illegitimate Assistance

Because of the serious penalties for plagiarism and illegitimate assistance at both the Program and University level, you should insure that any writing you submit—whether a draft or a final version—represents your own assertions and abilities and incorporates other texts in an open and honest manner. The best way to avoid plagiarism is to be careful to document your sources, even when you are only making use of data or ideas rather than an actual quotation. To avoid having your writing marked by illegitimate assistance, ask yourself whether you would be able, on your own and without further assistance, to revise and improve the writing in question. If the answer is "No"—if you would not be able to maintain the same conceptual and stylistic quality without outside assistance—then you should not submit the writing as your own work.

Other Types of Academic Dishonesty

In addition to matters of plagiarism and illegitimate assistance, there are several other types of academic dishonesty that are subject to strong university sanctions. They include, but are not limited to, the following:

1. Submitting a paper written by or obtained from another.

2. Using a paper or essay in more than one class without the expressed permission of the instructors involved.

3. Allowing another student to submit your work under his or her name.

There are serious penalties for plagiarism and other forms of academic dishonesty. In most cases, students receive an F for the course. Consult "Academic Dishonesty Sanction Guidelines" in the most recent version of *SCampus* for a complete listing of penalties.

The Writing Center

Taper Hall of Humanities (THH), Room 216

dornsife.usc.edu/writingcenter

General Information

The Writing Center provides free individual consultations and small-group workshops to assist students in improving their writing skills. Open to all members of the university community, the Writing Center is characterized by a nonjudgmental, comfortable environment; it is a friendly place where students can receive advice and suggestions at any stage of the writing process, from just getting started on a writing assignment to revising and editing a draft of a nearly completed essay. In fact, many students come to the Writing Center to talk about a writing assignment before they have written anything at all.

Dialogue is the essence of Writing Center pedagogy, and much of what takes place in a consultation is conversation, with both consultant and student asking questions and contributing to the discussion. Students usually know what they want to say, and consultants will help them express it in a way that suits their subject, audience, and purpose. Writing consultants are trained to work with students at all levels of their studies, and with both native and nonnative speakers of English; in all cases the goal is to help students improve as *writers*.

Writing Center Consultations

The aim of the Writing Center is to help students become better writers as they work on specific essays, not simply to improve that particular essay. Writing is approached as a *process* and consultations typically focus on *fostering skills* in such areas as thesis development and support, organization, rhetorical strategies, reader awareness, and use of sources and evidence, rather than focusing simply on correcting errors. Consultants can help students with surface errors and sentence-level issues, but the consultation is not a proofreading service. If you request assistance with surface editing, the consultant will generally help you edit a section of the essay (like a paragraph or single page), focusing primarily on helping you learn to identify the types of errors you may be making and discussing the necessary corrections; you can then apply what you have learned to the remainder of the paper yourself.

Preparing for a Writing Center Visit

You can derive the most benefit from a Writing Center conference and make the best use of the available time if you come prepared. The following ideas may be of use in planning your Writing Center visit:

1. **Make an Appointment.** Reservations for individual consultations and small-group workshops are made on the Writing Center website: dornsife.usc.edu/writingcenter. Appointment slots are limited and the Writing Center can be a very busy place, especially right before portfolios are due. You are welcome to stop by without a reservation to see if a drop-in consultation is possible, but without a reservation that is unlikely. Individual consultations are twenty-five minutes in length; workshops last for fifty minutes. When scheduling your appointment, be mindful of your assignment's due date and leave enough time to revise the essay following the consultation. Scheduling a consultation an hour or two before a paper is due does not allow time for significant revision.

2. **Know What You Want to Work On.** Writing Center consultations are generally most productive when you have thought in advance about what you would like to work on during your time with the consultant. Although it is fine for you to come to talk about an assignment before you begin writing, you are encouraged to begin *thinking* about your writing project *before* you come to the Writing Center. If you are in the beginning stage of working on a paper, you should review the assignment instructions carefully prior to the conference so that you will be able to ask questions about any part that confuses you, and perhaps engage in some preliminary brainstorming or other invention strategy prior to the conference. If you have written a draft, go through the draft and mark those areas with which you are least satisfied. A Writing Center conference involves collaborative work, so come into the Writing Center ready to participate. Bring the writing prompt or assignment instructions to show your consultant, and have a specific agenda in mind. Some agendas might be:

"I would like to discuss ideas for this paper."

"I would like to further develop the thesis statement for this paper."

"I would like to develop a counterargument for this paper."

"I would like to develop some relevant examples for this paper."

"I'd like to focus on incorporating some outside sources into this essay to support my argument."

"I am having difficulty with this introduction."

It is *not* useful to say:

"My teacher said I have to come to the Writing Center and here I am."

3. **Understand the Goals of Writing Center Instruction.** Because Writing Center instruction aims to help students become better writers, not simply to improve a particular paper, consultants will encourage you to be actively involved in the conference, to ask questions and take notes so that you can learn something that can be applied to subsequent writing tasks. Expect to participate fully in the conference, not simply to sit back and let the consultant do all the work. You will learn best when you do your *own* work.

You should also understand that Writing Center consultants usually focus on *global areas of writing* before addressing sentence level problems. In an initial Writing Center consultation, unless the paper is unusually well-developed, you will be encouraged to work on areas such as thesis development, support, and organization before working on issues such as spelling, punctuation, or grammar.

4. **Arrive Early.** You should arrive at least five minutes before your scheduled appointment to check in at the front desk. If you arrive more than five minutes late, you may find that your appointment time has been re-assigned to another student and you may need to reschedule.

Writing Center Workshops

Throughout the semester, the Writing Center offers fifty-minute "Grammar, Style and Skill Workshops" on a variety of subjects. These small-group workshops can contain up to eight students, and students are encouraged to bring their own writing projects to share and discuss in the workshop. Some of the workshop topics focus on specific problems of language usage characteristic of nonnative speakers of English, such as the usage of articles (a, an, the), understanding verb tenses, and basic sentence structure. Others focus on areas of writing more relevant to all academic writers, such as writing strong paragraphs, working with outside sources, or writing with clarity. Visit the Writing Center website (see address on page 147) for a complete list of workshops, including a detailed description and current schedule.